THE Cognac COMPANION

A CONNOISSEUR'S GUIDE

THE Cognac COMPANION
A CONNOISSEUR'S GUIDE

CONAL R. GREGORY

RUNNING PRESS
PHILADELPHIA · LONDON

Dedication

to Fiona

A QUINTET BOOK

9 8 7 6 5 4 3 2 1

Digit on the right indicates the number of this
printing

ISBN 0-7624-0195-8

Library of Congress
Cataloging-in-Publication Number
96-71134

This book was designed and produced by
Quintet Publishing Limited
6 Blundell Street
London N7 9BH

Creative Director: Richard Dewing
Art Director: Silke Braun
Designer: Ian Hunt
Senior Editor: Laura Sandelson
Editor: John Wright
Photographer: Paul Forrester

Typeset in Great Britain by
Central Southern Typesetters, Eastbourne
Manufactured in Singapore by Pica Graphics
Printed in Singapore by
Star Standard Industries (Pte) Ltd

This book may be ordered by mail from the publisher.
Please add $2.50 for postage and handling.
But try your bookstore first!

RUNNING PRESS
BOOK PUBLISHERS
125 South Twenty-second Street
Philadelphia Pennsylvania 19103-4399

Contents

NOTE

All references to gallons are to U.S. gallons. One U.S. gallon equals
0.03785 hectoliters and one imperial gallon equals 0.0456 hectoliters.
Hectoliters are the standard unit of measurement in the cognac industry.

PART I

The Story
of Cognac

"CLARET IS THE LIQUOR FOR BOYS;

PORT FOR MEN;

BUT HE WHO ASPIRES TO BE A HERO

MUST DRINK BRANDY."

Samuel Johnson must have had cognac in mind when he wrote this in April 1779. For elegance, depth of character, and style, cognac stands out as the finest grape brandy in the world. Yet its birthplace is little visited, and its making not fully appreciated.

The Cognac region–often referred to by historians as the "Saintonge," after the Gallic tribe of Santones–lies in western France, north of Bordeaux. The river Charente winds its way through the towns of Angoulême, Jarnac, Cognac, and Saintes to Rochefort and the Atlantic ocean.

Several Neolithic dolmen point to the region's long occupation. The Romans introduced the vine and salt extraction. Probus, Roman emperor from 276–282, extended vine cultivation to the region and by the twelfth century it was a noted area for wine production. As Dutch, Scandinavian, and English traders bought salt, a second commercial arm developed in wine.

How and why the region switched from a trade in wine to brandy is explained in different ways. Some consider that the low-alcohol wine deteriorated to such a degree on its sea voyage that traders from the Low Countries decided to distill it after landing. To answer this need, the French installed Dutch stills and started to deal in brandy. An alternative view is that brandy was purchased to add to the sailors' water to make it palatable! Certainly overproduction had resulted in thin, very light wines. With greater demand abroad for the local brandy, coupled with higher taxation on the river Charente from 1620–1650 (by comparison with the Gironde and the Loire), distillation developed quickly.

For the rest of the seventeenth century and through the eighteenth, new distillers emerged in the Cognac region–from noble landowner to

THE TOWN OF JARNAC, 1610

JEAN MARTELL (1694–1753), FOUNDER OF THE
OLDEST OF THE MAJOR COGNAC HOUSES.

village priest and humble peasant. Five vine varieties yielded prolific crops that proved excellent for brandy: Balzac, Blanche Ramée, Folle Blanche (by far the most popular), Gros Blanc, and Gros Bouillau. Cultivation was haphazard with vines planted about every 3 feet in every direction and without stakes or wire. If a vine withered, it was replaced by layering a healthy vine nearby. Mildew and other diseases were still unknown.

To the Charentes countryside, so different from its present orderly appearance, came several foreigners to develop the trade in brandy. James Delamain, son of the constable of Dublin Castle in Ireland, arrived in 1759, although his family had originally come from Jarnac. Jean Martell left Jersey in the Channel Islands for Cognac in 1715 while Richard Hennessy from Cork, Ireland, established his firm in 1765; the latter was already in the region as captain of an Irish brigade on the side of Louis XV. Thomas Hine left Dorset, England, for Cognac in 1782. The cofounder of Otard in 1799, Jean-Antoine Otard de la Grange, descended from a Scottish family that had followed James II into exile.

JEAN-ANTOINE OTARD DE LA GRANGE, COFOUNDER OF OTARD IN 1799.

THOMAS HINE (1755–1822), PROPRIETOR OF HINE AND
HIGHLY SKILLED IN THE ART OF DISTILLATION.

Gradually the stills improved and double distillation became the norm. The wood-fired boiler in a stone frame held about 53–79 gallons. As today, the head of the still was turban-shaped and the serpentine pipe, made of copper or terracotta, was inserted into the condenser, which was then often just a cask filled with water. To obtain around 67 percent alcohol–the maximum then permitted under English law to qualify for simple duty, because stronger brandy was subject to double duty–several consecutive heatings were required, either by redistilling the *brouillis* (the product of the first heating) or by adding it to a first stock of wine. In either case, only the middle portion of each heating was saved.

In the eighteenth and early nineteenth centuries, the cognac trade was largely in Protestant hands with their co-religionists abroad forming the base of a commercial network. The brandy, sold in casks, was "brown cognac" (sweetened with brown-syrup molasses, probably to cover up poor distillation) and "pale" (with no such addition).

Cognacs then started to be named according to their origin. "Champagne de Cognac" (referring to the chalky area centered on Segonzac) secured a higher price than brandy from the "Bois" (wooded area).

COPPER CHARENTE STILL DATING BACK TO THE NINETEENTH CENTURY.

Around 1850 the trading houses started to export in bottles, thereby gaining world-wide publicity and giving the consumer greater confidence. Glass production started in the town of Cognac and by 1880 sales of locally produced brandy reached one million cases (today it is about 12.1 million cases).

Yet the Cognac vineyards, then covering about 691,600 acres, were devastated by the aphid, *phylloxera*. It reached the region in 1878. The only vines that resisted were planted on the moist clay soils of the low-lands. By 1893, only about 98,800 acres remained in production. Gradually grafting onto American rootstock, which is *phylloxera*-resistant, took time. Two vine fungal diseases, mildew and oidium, also caused problems.

The overall result was to change vine cultivation. Planting in rows was developed, leaving room for plows or ox-drawn harrows, followed from 1950 by tractors. The space between rows was widened from about 2 to 6 feet, and stakes and wire were introduced.

IMPORTATION OF

BRANDY

Into the Port of New York

For the year ending Dec. 31, 1881

COMPILED FROM THE COLUMNS OF

BONFORT'S WINE AND SPIRIT CIRCULAR, OF JANUARY 10, 1882.

Brand.	Importer.	Gallons.
Otard, Dupuy & Co.	Cazade, Crooks & Reynand	64,575
Jas. Hennessy & Co.	Ed. Blackburn & Co.	54,705
Martell & Co	Renauld, Amy & Co.	41,775
A. Pellevoisin	G. Amsinck & Co.	20,000
Pinet, Castillon & Co.	Oswald Jackson & Bro.	24,319
Panat & Co.	Herm. Batjer & Bro.	20,271
Laurent & Marot	Cazade, Crooks & Reynaud	17,295
Jules Robin & Co.	E. LaMontague & Sons.	10,298
L. Furland & Co.	Emil Schultz	9,357
Vineyard Prop. Co.	Waldon & Co., Phila.	8,750
Sazerac de Forge & fils.	Ives, Beecher & Co.	7,682
Augier freres & Co	Luyties Bros	7,008
Gold Seal	B. W. Allen & Co.	6,750
Arzac Seignette	Walden & Co., Phila.	6,500
E. Remy-Martin & Co.	Albert Blum	5,847
Societe de Proprietaires.	M. Spiegel & Co	5,577
George Sayer & Co.	Chas. F. Schmidt & Peters.	5,408
Arzac Seignette	M. Lienan & Co.	4,700
La Grande Marque	L. Neuborn & Co.	4,051
F. Dessandier & Co.	E. & J. Burke.	3,722
Jules Duret & Co.	Robt. W. Tailor	3,612
Vineyard Prop. Co.	M. Lienan & Co.	3,560
J. Icenis, Hy. Monnie & Co.	I. H. Smith's Sons.	3,518
Dubois freres.	Brache, fils. & Co.	2,940
Arbouin, Marett & Co.	Paris, Allen & Co.	2,865
Vve. Robert & Co.	M. Spiegel & Co.	2,750
Barnett & fils	M. Spiegel & Co.	2,750
Roulliet & Delamain.	Runk & Unger.	2,740
W. Bertrand & Co.	P. W. Engs & Sons	2,600
J. E. Dulary & Co.	Purdy & Nicholas	2,488
Riviere, Gardrat & Co.	Dodge, Cammeyer & Co.	2,469
Comandon & Co.	Arguimbau, Wallis & Co.	2,424
Thos. Hine & Co.	G. Amsinck & Co.	2,080
Alexandre Matignon & Co.	Nicholas Bath & Co.	1,846
Barton & Guestier.	E. LaMontague & Sons.	1,644
A. Tibbot. fils & Co.	Julius Wilde & Bros	1,350
Various		112,061

Total gallons for the year 488,848

OFFICIAL STATISTICS OF IMPORTATION OF COGNAC INTO THE U.S. IN 1881.

LABELLING BOTTLES AT OTARD, EARLY 1900s.

Vines and the Vineyard

The boundaries for the area in which one can legally make cognac were decreed in May 1909 and subsequently amended. It extends along the banks of the river Charente, which becomes a wide, usually slow-flowing river and which was described by Henry IV as "the loveliest stream in my kingdom." The region covers most of the administrative *département* of Charente, all of Charente–Maritime, and small parts of Deux-Sèvres and Dordogne. In total, the delimited region is about 2.8 million acres of which around 1.7 million acres is classified as suitable for cultivation. Currently 203,454 acres are under vine.

The region has an average annual temperature of 56°F (70.7°F in summer, falling to 43.7°F in winter). Much of the rolling landscape has been compared to an English rural county.

At its heart lies a particularly chalky district, known as the Grande Champagne. Most critics feel that this yields the finest cognac with greater subtlety and more finesse than any other.

THE CHARENTE RIVER AT JARNAC.

VENDÉE

La Rochelle

Ile de Re

Aigre Fevi.

Ile D'Oleron

Rochefor

Marennes

Paris

FRANCE

Royan

ATLANTIC OCEAN

Grande Champagne	Fins Bois
Petite Champagne	Bons Bois
Borderies	Bois Ordinaires

VINEYARDS IN GRANDE CHAMPAGNE BELONGING TO RÉMY MARTIN.

Termed the *premier cru* (or first growth), the Grande Champagne district has 33,222 acres in production covering 27 parishes. The village of Segonzac is its center with the town of Cognac at its northwestern edge. A temperate microclimate is created by its position halfway between the Atlantic and the high ground of the upper Charente valley. Rich in calcium carbonate from the Cretaceous period (some 70–130 million years ago), this combination yields fine, delicate cognacs with a pronounced floral aroma, requiring long barrel aging to achieve maturity.

The second of the six districts, officially recognized in 1938, is the Petite Champagne, which forms an extensive semicircle around Grande Champagne. Its vines cover 39,196 acres, and it covers 60 parishes, taking in the towns of Archiac, Barbezieux, Châteauneuf-sur-Charente, and Jonzac. Like its more illustrious neighbor, the Petite Champagne enjoys a high chalky element and a good reputation.

When Grande Champagne and Petite Champagne are blended together, the resulting cognac can be described as "Fine Champagne," provided not less than half originated in the Grande Champagne district.

The Borderies is the smallest district of the six, covering just six parishes lying north of Cognac. Its vines cover a mere 10,063 acres, but its very rich soil—even with half the chalk content of that in Grande Champagne—and individual microclimate produce cognacs with an aroma reminiscent of violets. The cognac eau de vie matures more quickly and is much in demand in blends.

Three districts form the Bois: Fins Bois, Bons Bois, and Bois Ordinaires. Originally wooded, as the name suggests, the Bois was the area first cultivated for wine grapes until around 1650, as the Champagne districts were better for growing cereals.

The Fins Bois encircles the three districts of Grande and Petite Champagne and Borderies, as well as taking in a small area around the town of Mirambeau. Most of the district lies north and east of Cognac and includes the important towns of Angoulême and Saintes—278 villages in total. Its vines cover a far larger territory than any other: 83,177 acres, and they yield almost 40 percent of cognac production. On hard, limestone subsoil, the cognac is round, supple, and early maturing.

Clay with only a little chalk predominates in the Bons Bois, which surrounds the first four *crus*. To the west, its vines (such as around Cozes, Saujon, Talmont, and Tonnay-Boutonne) are influenced by the coastal climate. Some 30,292 acres are under vine. The cognac produced is fairly fast maturing and rather rough to taste.

VINEYARDS IN GRANDE CHAMPAGNE.

The sixth district, Bois Ordinaires or occasionally called Bois Communs, covers the outlying parts of the delimited Cognac region: mostly along the Atlantic (including the port of La Rochelle and town of Rochefort), the islands of Oléron and Ré, and a tiny area in the extreme southeast around St. Aulaye. Only 3,796 acres are under cognac vines, making it by far the smallest producing district. The quality is low and the farmers prefer fishing, gathering shellfish, and developing tourism. The distinctly sandy soil ensures fast-maturing cognac, much of which is sold to visitors.

Both red and white grape varieties are cultivated. In 1996, red vines covered 9,384 acres, white (for cognac) 203,454 acres, and other white 939 acres. This yielded 5.1 million gallons, 290 million gallons, and 536,254 gallons, respectively.

Production between the six districts is divided as follows:

DISTRICT	RED WINE GAL	WHITE WINE GAL	TOTAL GAL
Grande Champagne	124,921	47,572,588	47,697,509
Petite Champagne	336,842	58,941,777	59,278,618
Borderies	80,825	13,853,166	13,933,991
Fins Bois	1,736,810	121,405,510	123,142,320
Bons Bois	1,791,082	44,231,600	46,022,682
Bois Ordinaires	1,044,524	4,550,951	5,595,475
TOTAL	5,115,004	290,555,593	295,670,597

SOURCE: *1996 vintage (Bureau National Interprofessionnel du Cognac)*

Cognac's many small vinegrowers, numbering 18,824, grow a variety of grapes but concentrate on the Ugni Blanc, often referred to as the St. Emilion (but not to be confused with the Appellation in eastern Bordeaux of the same name). This vine is actually the most widely planted white grape in France but hardly ever features on a label. In Cognac, it is high-yielding with frequently up to 1,015 gallons per acre permitted. Ugni Blanc, known in Italy as Trebbiano, turns into a dry, highly acidic, rather thin wine that makes an ideal base for distillation, as well as for the region's famous sweet apéritif, Pineau des Charentes.

UGNI BLANC IS THE MAIN GRAPE OF COGNAC.

Ugni Blanc was probably first established in southern France when the Papal seat moved to Avignon (1308–1377), brought perhaps from Italy by Clement V or one of his successors. It replaced the main grape of cognac, the Folle Blanche, as it was far more resistant to fungal diseases.

Folle Blanche is still cultivated. It makes a relatively neutral wine. The third regional variety, Colombard, produces a rather less acidic, more alcoholic wine, which is less desirable from a distiller's point of view. It, too, suffers from oidium. Surplus Colombard production is sold as Vin de Pays Charentais.

When a district name, such as Borderies, is applied, up to 90 percent of the base cognac must come from these three varieties (Ugni Blanc, Folle Blanche, and Colombard), according to a decree of May 1936. Up to 10 percent can come from five other vine types: Blanc Ramé (sometimes called Meslier St. François and also found occasionally in the western Loire), Jurançon Blanc (also grown in small quantities at Montels in southwest France), Montils (yielding a well-

VINEYARDS NEAR CHATEAUNEUF.

TODAY HARVESTING BY HAND IS A RARE SIGHT.

rounded wine with aromas of exotic fruits like pineapple), Sémillon (widely grown around the world and, when blended with Sauvignon Blanc, makes Sauternes), and Sélect.

Surprisingly the Bureau National Interprofessionnel du Cognac (BNIC) does not maintain statistics on the different varieties grown. While Ugni Blanc is probably approaching 95 percent in most vineyards, smaller growers often hold on to their plantings of the unfashionable varieties. Montils, according to Christian Thomas at Château de Beaulon, is an old Armagnac vine that used to be tolerated by the Cognac authorities but is now recommended. He grows it for its lightness and finesse. Others ascribe pear and nutmeg aromas to Folle Blanche and lime blossom to the Colombard. Another reason for the drastic reduction in plantings of Folle Blanche since the nineteenth century is the difficulty in grafting it onto American rootstocks.

The days when vines were planted like currant bushes have gone, and mechanization has come to the Cognac region. In the past, all the local population was pressed into working the harvest, which officially began at Michaelmas (September 29). Then the grapes were placed in small wooden buckets (*bassiots*) and poured into tarred wicker baskets and finally into large vats on ox-drawn carts that transported the grapes to the farmhouse. A substantial wooden screw press yielded about 2.6 gallons per acre.

Today cognac vines are trained higher (frequently about 6 foot) and widely spaced (9.8–12.5 foot) apart. Most of the vineyards are now mechanically harvested with the grapes pressed either in horizontal plate presses or pneumatic presses. No addition of either acidity or sugar (chaptalization) is permitted during fermentation, which lasts about three weeks. The result is a weak, rather unappealing wine of 8 to 9 percent alcohol by volume—ideal for distillation.

LOADING THE HARVEST AT RÉMY MARTIN.

MECHANICAL HARVESTING OF GRAPES.

Distillation

C ognac is twice distilled using a traditional pot still, the same type as used for Scotch malt whisky. No time is wasted once the light wine has been fermented, as distillation has to be completed by March 31 following the harvest. The process continues day and night with distillers setting up camp beds in the still rooms, even spending Christmas Day and New Year's Day with the emerging brandy!

Three groups undertake the distillation: cooperatives (accounting for 75 stills with a volume of 82,415 gallons); *bouilleurs de profession*, who act for farmers as well as merchants (1,126 stills with 928,587 gallons); and *bouilleurs de cru*, individual farmers who also distill (1,674 stills with 923,684 gallons). Almost half the region's vine growers–9,600–also distill, with only about 200 professional distillers.

Copper is used for the still. The unfiltered wine, often still on the *lees* (the residue from the fermentation), is placed inside a bulb-shaped pot and heated, usually these days by natural gas. Gradually, alcoholic vapors rise and are collected in a cowl, which is shaped like an onion. Some compare the apparatus to a stretched pear, since a pipe runs off from the cowl to a coil that runs through a cooling tank to a collecting vat. The liquid after the first distillation is slightly cloudy and 27–30 percent alcohol by volume. It is known as *brouillis* or "low wine."

MARTELL'S DISTILLERY AT GALLIENNE IS ONE OF THE LARGEST IN THE REGION.

SPIRIT RUNS FROM THE COWL TO A COIL IN A PIPE
THROUGH A COOLING TANK INTO A COLLECTING VAT.

While up to 3,445 gallons may be distilled initially, a smaller still ensures a more stylish and less neutral spirit. Another variation is whether to use a *chauffe-vin* (heat exchanger) where the hot vapor warms the wine that is to be distilled, thereby reducing energy costs; some oxidation can occur, though.

EXTRACTING SOME OF THE LIQUID KNOWN AS *BROUILLIS* (LOW WINE) AT
THE END OF THE FIRST DISTILLATION.

STATE-OF-THE-ART DISTILLERY AT REMY MARTIN.

The second distillation (called *la bonne chauffe*) uses a still with a 795-gallon capacity but only up to 663 gallons can legally be filled. The process lasts about 12 hours and involves the distiller separating the very volatile elements that first vaporize (72 to 80 degrees) from the heart or middle part. He must also stop collecting the brandy once it falls below 60 percent, although in practice most houses will cut off earlier, even as high as 68 degrees to ensure a drier style.

The two parts rejected—called the "heads" and "tails"—are redistilled with the next batch of wine (ensuring a more neutral final spirit) or *brouillis* (thereby yielding a fruitier distillate). Again, houses vary on their practices. All agree that the care taken to separate the respective liquids should not be underestimated: it is the art of the distiller to secure the cleanest and most distinctive heart of the process. He relies on nothing more than the sensitivity of his taste buds and an alcoholometer. As Jean Fillioux in Grande Champagne says, "Only years of experience and know-how, based more often than not on a long family tradition, will ensure that he acts at precisely the right moment."

The Slow Maturation

The long aging given to cognac is unique among spirits. It allows the initial harsh tones to subside and for a mellow quality to develop through slow oxidation in the cask.

Some distillers prefer to age their brandy at the full strength it comes off the still, accepting a high evaporation rate. The French fiscal authorities permit a loss (poetically termed the "angels' share") of up to 3 percent. Really old cognacs may even be eventually bottled at the strength they naturally reach through time, but the vast majority are reduced soon after distillation by the addition of distilled water or a blend of cognac and water; the latter may be applied by stages so as not to cause too rapid a change.

THE WOOD FROM LIMOUSIN OAK TREES IS ONE
OF ONLY TWO TYPES USED TO MAKE THE AGING BARRELS.

THE COOPERAGE AT MARTELL.

The warehouse used for storing cognac ("cellar" is a misnomer as the buildings are above ground) has an effect. Many lie close to the river Charente and are consequently damp. Drier warehouses impart a harsher character to the brandy. A skillful cellarmaster will monitor the maturation process and move barrels from one building to another, sometimes placing them on the earth floor where the air is humid, and at intervals on the upper stories where the air is drier. In this way, he promotes the optimum development of both aroma and flavor.

The choice of wood—both age and type—is significant. Only oak from Quercus Robur and Quercus Petraea species may be used. Traditionally this has meant Limousin and Tronçais oak, using staves split from the trunk—not sawed—of trees that are usually 80–100 years old. Limousin grows east of Cognac around Limoges and imparts more tannin but less lignin (a hardening material which can give vanilla aromas) than Tronçais. The latter, from forests in central France, has closer grain and releases its tannin more quickly; it is popular therefore for cognacs intended for early sale.

Most barrels contain just over 92.5 gallons, but larger vats are used for blending. The staves are stored in the open for several years before being selected by the cooper. Few cognac houses maintain their own cooperages, but there is an impressive one at Renault Bisquit. At Hennessy, both their museum and video for visitors recreate brilliantly the craft of the *tonnellier* or cooper.

The choice of whether to use new wood for young brandy, or even for part of it, very much depends on the house style. Complex chemical changes take place during the aging, or as the French call it, *élevage*, derived from the verb "to breed." The new colorless spirit carries a fragrance of flowering vines as well as the innate character-istics of their region of origin. Some houses (like Frapin) consider new wood essential while a minority (such as Delamain) eschew its use.

In order to achieve uniformity, three additional materials may be added. *Boisé* (oak shavings infused in cognac) speeds the maturation process and compensates for brandy which is aged in large vats. Caramel is applied to adjust the color, and up to 1 ounce for every 4 quarts of sugar syrup can soften a blend.

Clearly there is a finite time a cognac may spend in the barrel before it becomes too woody. After seven years of contact, a barrel is called *barrique rousse* and retained for aging older brandies. Between 15 and 20 years of age, a cognac can acquire a fuller, fattier character, not unlike certain cheeses, and is termed *rancio*. With both a loss of volume and alcoholic strength comes a softer flavor and a concentration of aromas. Minute quantities of sugar (derived from cellulose in the wood) start to attain measurable levels.

The peak comes somewhere between 40 to 50 years of age. "After 60 years, a cognac has almost nothing more to gain from the wood and may well start to deteriorate with continued exposure to air," says Alain Braastad-Delamain, head of Delamain. Around this age, it is therefore transferred to large glass jars (or demijohns).

The oldest cognacs are held in a dark cellar, often away from other stock. Frequently this special reserve is called the "Paradis." The finest setting must be Château de Cognac—sometimes known as Château des Valois—where the future King François I was born in 1494. Here Otard maintains stocks dating from the 1820 vintage (of which three demijohns remain).

STAVES ARE STORED IN THE OPEN BEFORE BEING SELECTED
FOR USE BY THE COOPER.

SELECTING AND ASSEMBLING 32 STAVES THAT
WILL BE USED TO MAKE A BARREL.

PLACING THE BARREL OVER A FIRE GIVES IT A "TOASTY" QUALITY.

OAK CASK IN THE STORAGE CELLARS AT CHÂTEAU DE COGNAC.

THE CELLAR MASTER CHECKS THE MATURATION OF THE EAU-DE-VIE
AT CHÂTEAU DE COGNAC.

THE DARK AND SILENT AGING CELLAR AT CHÂTEAU DE COGNAC.

Aging, Blending, and the Label

The art of a cognac master blender is to see the raw spirit develop through its life, knowing when to change barrels and the optimum places for its maturation. Since practically all cognac is sold without a named vintage, the blender skillfully places cognacs of differing ages and districts together, achieving an overall harmony and consistency appropriate to the market.

The major houses purchase young spirit. Few own vineyards although members of the controlling or influential family behind the label may have some land under vine. Farmers develop a long-term relationship with particular houses and supply the raw spirit, much as their fathers and grandfathers had before them. Even with such regular sources of supply, blenders are not able to predict their forward requirements so many decades ahead. They therefore purchase more mature stocks and use their carefully nurtured reserves for both rounding off a stylish cognac and for their top-of-the-range deluxe brands.

The minimum age at which cognac may be sold to the public is 2.5 years, starting from October 1 in the year the grapes were picked. This is not an average age but the minimum cognac included in the blend.

Of course, this is the legal criteria, but leading blenders pride themselves on using considerably older stocks. However, their "formulas" are closely guarded secrets and will, in any case, develop with brand developments and public demand.

REFERENCE SAMPLES OF OLD COGNAC.

READING A LABEL

The actual terms used on labels are defined as:

- 🍂 VS or Three Star (★★★) is a blend where the youngest is not less than 2.5 years old.
- 🍂 VSOP (standing for Very Superior Old Pale), VO (Very Old), and Réserve have to be at least 4.5 years old.
- 🍂 Napoléon, XO, Extra, and Hors d'Age have to be a minimum 6 years old.
- 🍂 Fine Champagne is a blend of cognacs from the Grande Champagne and Petite Champagne districts comprising at least 50 percent from Grande Champagne.

Until recently, practically the only way to find a dated cognac—where a specific vintage is declared—was to buy "early landed" stock. This was young spirit, shipped from Cognac and matured in England. Delamain and Hine are the best known houses for this cognac. It is crucial to know that such cognac has been matured in good conditions and, of course, to be aware of the bottling date. Once cognac, like any spirit, goes into glass, it ceases to develop.

MASTER BLENDER AT HENNESSY.

BLUE GLASSES HIDE THE COLOR AND HAZE OF THE COGNAC

In 1988, the Bureau National Inter-professionnel du Cognac sanctioned a new method of recording the eventual date of a vintage on a label. It now allows single years of cognac to be stored away from other stocks under a double-lock system whereby entry has to be in conjunction with an official who holds the other key. Cognac controlled in this way may then be issued with a certificate proving the vintage date.

Glassware

The choice of glass in which to serve cognac is important. Cognac should be served in a glass which fits comfortably into the hand. Ideally it should be a thin-rimmed crystal glass. Avoid either too deep or overly narrow shapes of glasses. Contrary to restaurateur rumor, large "balloon" glasses are unsuitable as they release the brandy's elegant nose too violently "with the immediate effect of paralyzing one's sense of smell," says Alain Braastad-Delamain of Delamain.

The glass should be large enough to hold a good measure of cognac when filled one-third or one-quarter full. It should narrow slightly towards the top to trap the aromas and direct them towards the nose. The thinness of the glass is important in order that the subtle delicacy of the aromas can be slowly released through the gentle warmth of the hand.

COGNAC GLASSES

Cup the glass in the palm of one's hand, turning it slowly to release the delicious aromas. Even when the glass is empty, a fine fragrance will linger for several hours. Never warm a glass of cognac over a flame or hot water; the natural warmth of the hand is quite adequate.

Cognac glasses should be washed in clear, warm water without detergent, which can impart off flavors. Rinse the glass out with a drop of the same cognac just before tasting. Professional blenders incidentally use deep blue colored glasses so that they are not influenced either by color or any haze.

A cognac's color is not a reliable guide as to its age. The addition of caramel is permitted (within regulated levels) as a coloring agent. This can be abused to make a young cognac appear much older than its true age but is reasonable if the purpose is to ensure color consistency for a brand where a minimal caramel addition is required.

Tasting Cognac

*I*nitially examine the appearance: does the depth of color accord with the quality designation? Depth of color (i.e. more tawny than mid-straw in the center) suggests greater aging but this could have been achieved through the addition of caramel.

To judge the nose, hold the glass at a slight distance and gradually bring it closer to one's nose. Warmed to the right temperature, a good cognac releases a pleasant, immediate freshness and balanced fruityness. When aged in a barrel, cognac acquires aromatic complexity, reflecting spicy tones and wood/vanilla characteristics. At its most complex, a cognac shows the *rancio* style that is really sought after.

On the palate, take very small amounts, allowing prolonged enjoyment without over-consumption of alcohol. A cognac can "fan out" in the mouth if one chews it with closed lips. Try "whistling in," as some tasters say: purse the front lips, draw air in through the side of the mouth, and taste the cognac at the back of one's mouth where the sensitive taste buds are located. The flavor should fill the back palate. The finer and longer the taste remains, the better the "finish." An unbalanced and/or too youthful cognac will appear to be fiery without the softening tones and added dimension acquired with age.

WARM THE BRANDY BEFORE TASTING IT.

FIRST EXAMINE THE APPEARANCE.

YANN FILLOUX, CELLAR MASTER AT HENNESSY, JUDGES THE NOSE.

Unlike wine, cognac does not improve in the bottle. Cognac bottles should be stood upright to prevent the brandy from acquiring cork taint. Really old cognacs are sensitive to the cold, which may cause them to become cloudy. They are best stored at room temperature, away from the light. Finally, do not leave a bottle of uncorked cognac for longer than the time required to fill a glass otherwise it will evaporate.

Top-quality cognacs really round off a good meal. Personally I prefer them served around 40 percent alcohol by volume, which is the usual bottling strength. However, it is fine to add a little pure water if this is more to your taste.

In cooking, the combined aromas and flavors of cognac enhance many dishes, particularly when flambéed (as with crêpes Suzette and lobster). Cognac can also replace lemon juice or vinegar when making a mayonnaise. Try also adding a dash to sauces and gravies; it seems to work particularly well with duck and goose. Cognac adds another dimension to a dessert, whether a light mousse or a fresh fruit salad.

COCKTAILS MADE WITH COGNAC

Cognac's concentrated aroma of grapes and oak, combined with mellow richness on the palate, unite to make it a most appealing base for cocktails. Try the following, using VS or VSOP brands:

- As a long drink with water (called *Fine á l'eau* in French).
- Mixed with soda water.
- Horse's Neck: cognac mixed with ginger ale, a twist of lemon peel, and a dash of Angostura Bitters (the latter is actually rum-based and now comes from Trinidad); ensure it is a drier cognac if the sweeter American ginger ale is used.
- Mixed with tonic water; however, some consider the quinine in the tonic does not harmonize with the cognac.
- Cognac Sour: cognac mixed with fresh lemon juice and sugar syrup.
- Sidecar: 2 ounces cognac, 0.25 ounce Cointreau, 0.5 ounce lemon juice—all shaken and decorated with a twist of lemon peel.
- One-third cognac to two-thirds fresh orange juice, poured over three large ice cubes and decorated with a slice of orange.

Cuisine of Cognac

The regional food starts with Pineau des Charentes, an appealing medium-sweet apéritif that is also used in certain dishes. Pineau is fresh grape juice (either white or rosé) to which young cognac is added to stop fermentation. This combination is then aged in oak barrels for one year and sold at an alcoholic level of 16–22 percent. Pineau has its own Appellation, dating from October 1945. It is not unlike *ratafia* (which is made in the Champagne region) but fresher. Serve it chilled.

Seafood is popular. Oysters from Marennes can be served with hot garlic sausages. Clams, mussels, and scallops are plentiful. *Lavagnons Charentais* (clam-like shellfish) are usually simply cooked with chopped onions reduced to a purée to which strained water is added from the *lavagnons* (which have been cooked separately); add a little butter, parsley and season. Serve hot.

NORMANDIN-MERCIER PINEAU DES CHARENTES.

Mussel stew (*mouclade*) is made with cream, Pineau des Charentes, and shallots. *Chaudrée* is the regional equivalent of bouillabaisse, taking its name from the caldron in which the stew is cooked. The base is often cuttlefish; eel, sole, and other fish regularly form part of the recipe.

The snail that feeds on the cognac vines, the *cagouille*, can be served in puff-pastry with garlic and herbs. It can also be used in a stew (*lumas*) with local wine, shallots, and garlic. The latter is a specialty of La Rochelle.

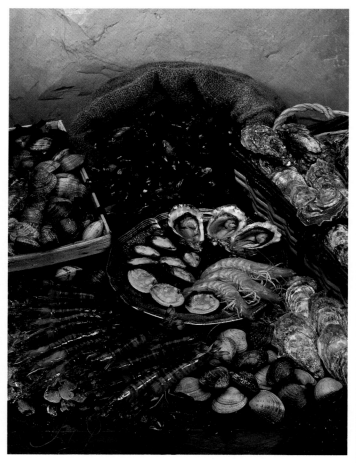

MUSSELS, OYSTERS, AND CLAMS ARE POPULAR AND CAN EASILY
BE FOUND IN MARENNES.

THE HIGHLY PRIZED CHARENTAIS MELON.

Charentais melon (often with a generous dash of Pineau des Charentes served inside it) and *grillons Charentais* (a fatty goose or pork terrine) make good starters.

Apart from local mushrooms, the other outstanding vegetable of the region is the white haricot bean (*mojette*). It is served in a stew with lamb, carrots, and onions.

Poultry is found on many menus. The local chicken, *Poule de Marans*, is said to be a cross between a local variety and a breed from the Far East. It is fat with fine flesh. The best known game dish, *Nid de Cailles au Pineau*, is quail cooked in Pineau des Charentes with streaky bacon and Muscatel grapes; truffle slices are often added.

Much of the cooking uses Charentais butter, which is said to be the best in France, even superior to that from Normandy; it has a slightly nutty taste. Like the local sweet melons, it has its own Appellation. The butter is particularly good around Surgères, north of the town of Cognac.

One of the novel country dishes, often served at Christmas, is *sauce de pire*: cooked pork blood with a thick viscous sauce, served with fried potatoes.

GOAT CHEESE IS A LOCAL DELICACY, AS IS *MOTTIN CHARENTAIS* AND *LA PIGOUILLE*.

Limousin beef and *pré salé* lamb (from the coastal pastures) are both of high quality. In cheese, *Mottin Charentais* is from cows' milk and looks like a squat Camembert but slightly taller. *La Pigouille*, again using cows' milk, contains at least 50 percent fat and is matured in oak leaves. The name originates from a pole used to propel flat-bottomed boats along the Charente river. For a local goat cheese that is creamy white, round, and soft, look for *Le Petit Semussec*, which originates from the village of the same name, lying between Cozes and Royan.

The Cognac people enjoy their desserts. *Galette Charentaise* is a flat cake, using self-rising flour, eggs, sugar, butter, salt, and vanilla essence. It is not a type of crêpe, as in other regions, but a cross between sponge cake and shortbread. Baked into a thin disk about nine inches in diameter, it is usually flavored with angelica and lemon. *Caillebotte* is a cheesy form of yogurt, like uncooked cheesecake, often served with cognac poured over it and sometimes accompanied by chives.

Cognac-flavored ice cream (*Parfait au Cognac*) and *Sabaillon* can be delicious, particularly in summer.

Finally, the region is known for an unusual bread, the *torteau*. Baked into a flat oval shape, it is cut several times across the middle, suggesting a barred window. It looks like Arab bread.

COGNAC IS FAMED FOR ITS ARRAY OF DELICIOUS DESSERTS, ESPECIALLY *CAILLEBOTTE* WHICH IS SIMILAR TO CHEESECAKE.

Cognac for the Visitor

From the sandy beaches around Royan and sailing around the islands to the Romanesque churches and historic towns, the visitor to Cognac country will find an infinite variety of interests. Many cognac houses open their doors and even have special facilities (as set out in the cognac directory which follows). Sports enthusiasts will find canoeing, cycling, fishing, golf (such as the 18 holes at St. Brice), horse riding, squash, and tennis.

The town of Cognac makes a good base. Mentioned in the ninth century, it was fortified in the Middle Ages. During the Hundred Years' War of 1337–1453 (which arose out of the English monarchy's claim to the French crown), Cognac was at times "English" and on occasion "French." Under the patronage of the Valois-Angoulême family, it became a prosperous economic center. It was the birthplace of both Francis I (1494), who became king of France in 1515, and Jean Monnet (1888), one of the fathers of modern Europe.

EQUESTRIAN STATUE OF THE FAMOUS FRENCH KING, FRANCIS I.

Cognac is home to several fine brandy houses as well as the bottle-making plant of St. Gobain, which is the largest in the world, producing 2 million bottles a day. The narrow winding streets that rise up from the banks of the Charente river house many old buildings.

PLACES TO VISIT IN COGNAC

- ❦ Château des Valois, whose walls date from the thirteenth century; see Count John's Tower and the vaulted room (La Salle des Gardes).
- ❦ St. Léger church: Romanesque church with beautiful Gothic rose window.
- ❦ Cognac Museum (48 bd Denfert Rochereau) contains regional ceramics, archaeological finds (including a Neolithic canoe), sculpture, and a reconstructed Charentais interior from around 1875; see the section devoted to Cognac production.
- ❦ Cognac Houses: Camus, Hennessy, Martell, and (just over 3 miles from the center) Rémy Martin.

Several festivals are held each year: police films (early April), jazz (early August), and European literature (early November).

CHÂTEAU DE COGNAC STANDS ON THE BANK OF THE CHARENTE RIVER.

Jarnac, to the east of Cognac, is a sleepy town, again lying on the Charente river. President Mitterrand was born there. Courvoisier, Delamain, and Hine age their stocks here. The eleventh century St. Peter's church has murals of the same age at the base of the bell tower.

THE CHARENTE RIVER AT JARNAC.

Segonzac, lying at the heart of the Grande Champagne district, has a damaged Romanesque church with a twelfth-century tower and fifteenth-century choir. Frapin is based there.

Angoulême is a major center, lying east of Cognac at the junction of the N10 and N141.

PLACES TO VISIT IN ANGOULÊME

- Museum of Fine Arts, housed in the twelfth-century former bishop's residence. This is the most important provincial collection of African art, as well as sixteenth- to eighteenth-century weapons, fine ceramics (Sazerac, Fleurat, Jucaud among aothers), and French neoclassical paintings.
- St. Peter's Cathedral: Romanesque from 1102–1136 with magnificent façade showing scenes of Christ's Ascension and the Last Judgment.
- Covered market (*Les Halles*), built by Edouard Warin in 1888, overlooking the old commercial heart of the town.
- Town hall: former fortified castle with two remaining towers, a thirteenth-century keep and fifteenth-century round tower; inside see the grand staircase and Second Empire-style drawing rooms.
- Chapel of Franciscan nuns (rue de Beaulieu) with its thirteenth-century Gothic nave, fourteenth-century square chancel, and tomb of the writer Balzac, who was born in Angoulême in 1597.
- National Comics & Image Center: the only comic-book museum in France to display comic plates exclusively, housed in a former brewery beside the river Charente.
- Le Nil Paper Museum: a working paper museum of papermaking and paper art.

Walk around the ramparts for magnificent views, 230 feet above the river. Take a boat down the Charente to find a traditional paper mill, a distillery, a cognac warehouse, and a chocolate factory.

Saintes is a delightful old town and makes an alternative base to Cognac. Lying on an important road from Lyons, it was the capital of Aquitaine for about a century.

ARCH OF GERMANICUS AT SAINTES.

PLACES TO VISIT IN SAINTES

- Arch of Germanicus, erected early in the first century at the entrance to the bridge which crossed the Charente.
- Gallo-Roman amphitheater and remains of the Roman baths, which overlook the old town.
- St. Eutrope: built by Benedictine monks and consecrated in 1096, becoming an important stopping point for pilgrims on their way to Santiago de Compostela in Galicia; see the beautiful carved capitals and the crypt.
- St. Peter's Cathedral in the Gothic style and an unfinished belfry which is 190 feet high; fine organ; each summer the church treasure is exhibited in the chapter house.
- Musée du Présidial (rue Victor-Hugo) was founded in 1864 and houses Flemish and Dutch art (Coignet, Floris Schooten) and seventeenth- and eighteenth-century French (Rigaud, Allegrain), with a room devoted to Saintonge ceramics.
- Musée Dupuy-Mestreau (rue Monconseil) is a fine example of eighteenth-century architecture, housing the private collections of Abel Mestreau (1855–1939), including costumes, headdresses, arms, and a peasant's kitchen/living room.
- Musée de l'Echevinage (rue Alsace-Lorraine) is the former town hall. Nineteenth- and twentieth-century art includes genre and oriental subjects.
- Some 100 coins from Sèvres are unusual.

Jonzac lies south of Cognac on the border between the Petite Champagne and Fins Bois districts. A former Huguenot town built on a rocky spur over the river Seugne, Jonzac has an underground thermal spa. See the fifteenth-century door of the château, restored sixteenth-century convent, archaeological museum, and nearby Château de Meux.

La Rochelle is famous for its old harbor and three outstanding medieval towers. A haven of style with lively quayside markets, the town was given to the English by Eleanor of Aquitaine upon her marriage to Henry II (but eventually lost in the Hundred Years' War). See the ornate town hall, which houses Henri Motte's painting of the town's blockade by Richelieu. Under a mile to the south is a marina (Port des Minimes) with an internationally famous aquarium that has a shark chamber.

Several festivals take place at La Rochelle, including international film (summer) and music, Les Francofolies (mid-July). The neighboring islands of Oléron and Ré are within the Cognac Appellation. Ré was only linked to the mainland in 1988 by a humpback toll bridge. Salt is still extracted. Visit quiet St. Marie, whose tiny streets have hardly been affected by the twentieth century, nature reserve (for barnacle geese and wading birds like the avocet and plover), and animal park (Arche de Noé, or Noah's Ark) at St. Clément.

Oléron has fine oyster beds and an oyster museum at Le Château, as well as a Romanesque church at St. Georges. Le Grand-Village displays a peasant homestead and a traditional costume museum.

THE MARINA IN LA ROCHELLE.

Rochefort (lying half way between Saintes and La Rochelle) is an old port where the river Charente becomes tidal. It is also known for its thermal spa.

PLACES TO VISIT IN ROCHEFORT

- ❦ Royal rope factory, built in the seventeenth century, with exhibitions on rope-making, shipbuilding, and sailing.
- ❦ Dry-dock reconstruction of the French ship Hermione, which served during the American Revolution.
- ❦ Maritime museum in Hôtel Cheusses houses seventeenth- and eighteenth-century model ships.
- ❦ Musée d'Art et d'Histoire houses African, Asian, and Oceanic collections.
- ❦ Métiers de Mercure Museum recreates historic town scenes.

Aulnay in the Bons Bois, north of Cognac, has the splendid church of St. Peter, a leading example of Poitou Romanesque architecture. The sculptures on the façade depict the crucifixion of St. Peter, Christ in majesty, the months, signs of the zodiac, and the wise and foolish virgins.

CHURCH OF ST. PETER IN AULNAY.

THE TWELFTH-CENTURY CHURCH OF ST. RADEGONDE IN TALMONT.

Pons lies southwest of Cognac in the Fins Bois district. Its keep and ramparts overlook the meandering river Seugne, which flows into the Charente. Both St. Vivien church and the pilgrims' hospice are worth a visit. To the north lies the charming Château de la Roche-Courbon, sometimes referred to as the home of Sleeping Beauty. It is a magnificent fifteenth- to sixteenth-century property with formal gardens. Inside see the gallery of paintings on wood, the Louis XIII room, guards' room, kitchen in the style of the region, and a small museum of prehistory in the keep.

St. Jean d'Angély lies north, northwest of Cognac on the road to Santiago on the site of a Roman villa. Today the towers of the former abbey, the Pollory fountain, clock tower, and fine wooden-fronted houses of the fifteenth- and sixteenth-centuries lend a charming air. The town's museum has both archaeological exhibits and memorabilia associated with the early days of Citroën. Not far away lies the Châteaux of Beaufief and Fenioux, noted for its fine Romanesque church.

Surgères, north of Saintes, has a lovely château, but also both a twelfth-century church (Notre Dame) with an octagonal bell tower and sculptured façades, and a seventeenth-century town hall.

Talmont lies southeast of Royan. The village was once part of a Roman town which disappeared into the sea through coastal erosion. Now the twelfth-century church of St. Radegonde stands on low cliffs right at the edge of the Gironde estuary. There is a small museum in the former village school. Today Talmont and its 75 inhabitants accept some 200,000 summer visitors.

PART II

The Cognac Directory

A. E. AUDRY

Jean BALLUET

Paul BEAU

Château de BEAULON

BERTRAND et Fils

BONNIN

CAMUS

CCG
BRUGEROLLE
MEUKOW

CHABASSE

Dominique
CHAINIER et Fils

COURVOISIER

CROIZET

A. de LUZE

GASTON de LAGRANGE

L. de SALIGNAC

DEAU

DELAMAIN

DOMPIERRE

A. E. DOR

DUBOIGALANT

A. E. DUPUY

EXSHAW

Jean Luc FERRAND

Pierre FERRAND

Jean FILLIOUX

Alain FOUGERAT

P. FRAPIN

GABRIEL et ANDREU

GAUTIER

Paul GIRAUD

GODET Frères

Léopold GOURMEL

GOURSAT-GOURRY
de Chadeville

GUERBÉ

A. HARDY

JAS. HENNESSY

Thomas HINE

Edgard LEYRAT

Guy LHÉRAUD

J & F MARTELL

Jean-Paul MAURIN

MENARD et Fils

MENUET

J. Y. & F. MOINE

Château MONTIFAUD

MOYET

J. NORMANDIN-MERCIER

OTARD

J. PAINTURAUD

Château PAULET

André PETIT et Fils

PLANAT

PRUNIER

RAGNAUD-SABOURIN

Raymond RAGNAUD

RÉMY MARTIN

RENAULT BISQUIT

L. ROYER

M. TIFFON

TRIJOL

UNICOOP
MOUNIER

PRINCE HUBERT DE POLIGNAC

A. E. AUDRY

La Fief Gallet, Pessines, 17450 Thénac
tel: (33-5) 46 92 65 38
Visitors by appointment

A. E. Audry was founded in 1878 by the great-great-grandfather of the current owner. From the beginning, they concentrated on very old cognacs. However, 40 years ago, upon the death of Aristide Boisson, who had married Odette Audry in 1905, the company stopped selling, although it retained some old stocks.

In 1976, Bernard Boisson, the present owner and grandson of Aristide Boisson, revived the business. Four cognacs are now available, largely based on old reserves but with small quantities purchased from the Grande and Petite Champagne districts and the Fins Bois.

Tasting Notes

AUDRY RÉSERVE SPÉCIAL FINE CHAMPAGNE
(PACKED IN INDIVIDUAL WOODEN BOX)

Amber hue; delicate, soft, fruity nose; elegant soft, fruity palate; many layers; mid-length. **Very good.**

AUDRY MÉMORIAL FINE CHAMPAGNE
(42 PERCENT ALCOHOL)
(PACKED IN INDIVIDUAL WOODEN BOX)

Amber hue; delicate appealing, lovely fruit on nose, apricots; palate shows lovely style; good fruit; long length; spirity finish.
Very good to exceptional.

AUDRY RÉSERVE SPÉCIAL FINE CHAMPAGNE.

The Audry Réserve Spéciale Fine Champagne is a blend evenly divided between the Grande and Petite Champagne districts from the 1972 and subsequent vintages. It was blended in 1989 after aging in new Limousin oak. Audry says it has a hint of cinnamon and vanilla on the nose and that the wood "is understated and well-integrated."

Their Mémorial Fine Champagne, sold at 42 percent alcohol, has a base of Grande Champagne (38 percent 23–30 years and 20 percent over 35 years) and 33 percent Petite Champagne (25–30 years), topped

- RANGE -

NAPOLÉON FINE
CHAMPAGNE

RÉSERVE SPÉCIALE
FINE CHAMPAGNE

MÉMORIAL FINE
CHAMPAGNE

LOT CINQ MILLE
GRANDE
CHAMPAGNE

up with old reserve stock (Grande Champagne 5 percent over 45 years and 2 percent over 60 years with 2 percent Petite Champagne over 50 years). This fully mature blend was launched in 1984. Boisson says, "Mémorial is the very quintessence of its noble origins and has its own strong personality." The blending is undertaken three years prior to bottling in a 2,650-gallon wooden vat, but the final aging in 9,275-gallon barrels which have previously contained the oldest cognac.

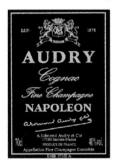

The Napoléon Fine Champagne has a base of Grande Champagne (25 percent over 20 years and 20 percent over eight years) and Petite Champagne (20 percent each of over eight and 15 years, respectively); to this, small older stocks are added: 10 percent Petite Champagne over 25 years and 5 percent Grande Champagne over 30 years).

Audry also offers a blend of Grande Champagne cognacs of 40–50 years age under the name "Lot Cinq Mille."

Annual sales are 15,000–20,000 bottles to leading restaurants and specialist retailers. Expect to find Audry Cognacs outside France in the U.S., Japan, Australia, Austria, and Germany.

Jean BALLUET

LE BOURG, 1 RUE DES ARDILLÈRES,
17490 NEUVICQ-LE-CHÂTEAU
TEL: (33-5) 46 26 64 74

*Visitors (except September 10–30 and before the harvest in October) from
8.00AM–12 noon and 2.00–5.00PM. From the square tower in the village,
there are splendid views across to Cognac and the surrounding countryside.*

*L*ying at Neuvicq-le-Château in the Fins Bois district between Matha and Rouillac (just south of the N139), the Balluet vineyard is mostly planted in Ugni Blanc with just a little Colombard and Folle Blanche. The Balluets are one of the oldest families in the village and have been distilling since 1845. The old still from that time remains but is no longer used. A new pot still has taken over.

- RANGE -

VSOP

TRÈS VIEILLE
RÉSERVE

NAPOLÉON

HORS D'AGE

XO

BALLUET VSOP.

Neither grapes nor wine are purchased additionally. Its annual production is 159,000 gallons wine, most of which is distilled but some made into Pineau des Charentes. VSOP sells about 7,000 bottles, Très Vieille Réserve about 4,000, and Napoléon, Hors d'Age, and XO about 1,500.

New oak barrels are purchased each year from major coopers, like Seguin Moreau. Balluet's cognac is aged half in Limousin oak and half in Tronçais. Its major markets are France, Germany, and the U.K.

Tasting Notes

VSOP

Fine, pale lemon hue; fruity, spirity nose; palate shows prunes; fair fruit; rather fiery finish; mid-length. **Fair.**

BALLUET TRÈS VIEILLE RÉSERVE
(PRESENTED IN FROSTED BOTTLE)

Pale tawny core with long pale ocher rim; stylish mellow fruit and walnuts on nose with no harsh tones; palate shows soft fruit, light woody character, mid length, balanced. **Good to very good.**

BALLUET TRÈS VIEILLE RESERVE.

Paul BEAU

RUE MILLARDET, 16130 SEGONZAC
TEL: (33-5) 45 83 40 18
Visitors by appointment

*S*amuel Beau, Paul's father, founded the business at the end of the nineteenth century. He expanded the vineyard and erected the main buildings. He died before World War I and was succeeded by Paul and his wife, Denise, who came from an established vinegrower's family. Paul Beau has mainly concentrated on the aging process for his cognac stocks. Since 1977, cognac under the "Paul Beau" label has been available. Its Hors d'Age, aged for 20–25 years, is sold at 43 percent alcohol, while the Vieille Réserve is 12–15 years old and "very characteristic of cognac's Premier Cru qualities," according to Beau; the latter is sold at 40 percent alcohol. A Borderies Extra-Vieilles is over 40 years old and sold in strictly limited amounts in numbered bottles at 44 percent alcohol.

- **RANGE** -

BORDERIES EXTRA-VIEILLES

HORS D'AGE VIEILLE GRANDE CHAMPAGNE

VIEILLE RÉSERVE GRANDE CHAMPAGNE

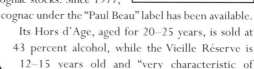

Tasting Note

HORS D'AGE VIEILLE GRANDE CHAMPAGNE

Mid-tawny core; peaches and fruit on nose; real style on palate, showing good inviting fruit, smooth with length. **Very good.**

VIEILLE GRANDE CHAMPAGNE.

Château de BEAULON

B.P. 1, 17240 Saint-Dizant-du-Gua
TEL: (33-5) 46 49 96 13
Visitors 9.00AM–12 noon and 2.00–6.00PM: May–September, every day;
October–May, Monday–Friday

Historic Château de Beaulon lies in a small enclave of the Fins Bois, southwest from Jonzac, off the N730 road between Mirambeau and Royan. The house was built in 1480 by two aristocratic families, the De Vinsons and De Beaulons, at the end of Louis XI's reign. In 1672, the Archbishop of France inherited the estate and gave it to the bishops of Bordeaux to use as their summer residence.

Cognac was first distilled at the property in 1712 by Louis-Amable de Bigot, following his re-acquisition of Château de Beaulon from the Church. Succeeding generations of families—Bremond d'Ars, La Porte, and Savignac des Roches—have maintained the tradition, which is today passionately upheld by the present owner, Christian Thomas.

Thomas both maintains tradition (such as continuing with the unusual, indeed obscure, Montils grape variety) and eschews modern chemical treatments in favor of bioculture.

The vineyard covers 210 acres of which almost 156 acres are planted with grapes for cognac, the balance being for Pineau des Charentes. On distinctly chalky soil, four cognac grapes are grown: almost 62 acres Colombard, 39.5 acres Folle Blanche, 37 acres Ugni Blanc, and 17.3 acres Montils. The latter is some 90 years old. Thomas says Montils is an old Armagnac vine, imparting a lighter style

CHÂTEAU DE BEAULON COGNAC RARE.

with good finesse to cognac. Once tolerated by the cognac authorities, it is now recommended, says Thomas.

Thomas believes that his cognac can achieve greater complexity by using several grape varieties. Rather than rely exclusively on the relatively high-yielding Ugni Blanc, the other grapes impart subtlety and a richness to the aromas.

He prefers to use fish fertilizer from La Rochelle and avoids chemical substitutes, pesticides, and synthetic weed killers. Seventeen work on the land, achieving a yield of 1,240 gallons per acre instead of 1,442 gallons per acre yield for the region. The level that can typically be used for cognac is 748 gallons per acre, although this can be higher (such as in 1995 when it was 961 gallons/acre).

The cognac grapes are mechanically harvested, apart from the oldest vines which are hand-picked; this is in contrast to the Pineau vines (Sémillon, Cabernet Sauvignon, Merlot, Sauvignon Blanc, and Cabernet Franc) which are hand-picked. The fermentation yields an above average alcoholic strength of 10 percent (actually 11.8 percent in some years, like 1996) against a regional average of 8.5 percent.

MINIATURE VERSIONS OF VSOP AND XO.

Beaulon uses only its own grapes; neither grapes nor wine is purchased in. Distillation commences after the second or malolactic fermentation in one of four stills: two take 398 gallons and two take 610 gallons. The varieties are separately distilled and only blended together as spirits. Thomas distills on the *lees* and preheats the wine in a *chauffe-vin*. The first distillation takes 11 hours and the second at least 14 hours.

Only new Limousin oak is used, each barrel taking 73–106 gallons, for the first six to seven months. Then the spirit, which is not reduced in strength at this stage, is transferred into older wood. After three years, Beaulon uses a cognac-and-water mix of 24 percent alcohol to reduce the VS and VSOP styles to 58–60 percent alcohol by volume. A real harmony is achieved by Thomas in blending Beaulon cognacs of different ages. On a visit in 1996, he had stock going back to 1907 in glass and to 1959 still in wood. Thomas prefers not to date the final cognac with a single year "as it would be too easy to obtain—as in Armagnac." Certainly this single estate, using traditional methods and old vine varieties with small stills, makes stylish cognac.

Château de Beaulon has been a prize winner with gold medals on no less than four occasions at the Paris Fair (1972, 1973, 1975, and 1976). In 1991, it achieved the Citadelle d'Or Trophy at Vinexpo, and in 1994 at the World Wine Competition in Brussels it won a diploma of honor. Beaulon has the royal warrants for the courts of Belgium and Denmark

- **RANGE** -

THREE STAR

VSOP

NAPOLÉON

XO

GRANDE
FINE EXTRA

COGNAC RARE

and is the appointed supplier to many embassies. It can be found in leading restaurants and such outlets as Harrods in London and Fauchon in Paris.

In the grounds, there is a historic dovecot, while the park is known for its "blue fountains," rich natural springs whose still, clear waters mirror a strange dark-blue color beneath centuries-old trees.

Apart from cognac, Beaulon makes award-winning Pineau des Charentes, sold at five and 10 years. Lightly chilled, it is delicious poured into melon (in place of the ubiquitous port) and to accompany light desserts, as well as soft and crumbly white cheeses. It shows sweet fruit and is mid-length on the finish.

SOUTH SIDE OF THE FIFTEENTH-CENTURY CHÂTEAU DE BEAULON.

Tasting Notes

CHÂTEAU DE BEAULON NAPOLÉON
(NUMBERED EMBOSSED BOTTLES)

Deep amber appearance; delicate, floral, fruity nose, stylish; palate shows walnuts, elegant fruit, many layers, fair acidity; good length, balanced.
Very good.

GRANDE FINE EXTRA
(NUMBERED EMBOSSED BOTTLES)

Mid-ocher hue with wide, pale rim; delicate, floral fruit on nose with no harsh tones; light, soft, many-layered taste, smooth, showing real style.
Very good.

BERTRAND et Fils

DOMAINE DES BRISSONS DE LAAGE, RÉAUX,
17500 JONZAC
TEL: (33-5) 46 48 09 03
Visitors daily

*D*omaine des Brissons de Laage dates from 1731. Lying in the Petite Champagne district at Réaux, northeast of Jonzac, the Bertrand family holding covers 173 acres of vineyards, entirely composed of Ugni Blanc vines. About 13,250 gallons pure alcohol is distilled annually from 265,000 gallons wine.

Two stills, each able to hold 663 gallons, are on site. New wood from both Limousin and Tronçais is bought from the cooperages of Yves Pelletan and Seguin Moreau.

BERTRAND VSOP PETIT FINE CHAMPAGNE

A reserve stock of 132,500 gallons cognac is maintained, as well as 79,500 gallons Pineau des Charentes for a white and rosé.

Bertrand's awards include the Grand Prix Foire de Liège in 1905 and in Bordeaux in 1907. More recently, they secured the Lauréat de la Cuvée in 1985 to celebrate the 50th anniversary of the Appellation Cognac.

- RANGE -

THREE STAR

SELECTION 5 STAR

VSOP

VSOP RÉSERVE

NAPOLÉON

VIEILLE RÉSERVE

XO

BERTRAND VSOP

Tasting Notes

BERTRAND VSOP

Mid-tawny core with distinct mid-straw rim; nose shows rich good autumnal fruits; supple, fruity taste, short length, fiery finish. **Fair to good.**

BERTRAND VSOP PETITE FINE CHAMPAGNE

(WITH NECK SEAL OF THEIR TRADEMARK, A WINDMILL)

Mid-tawny core with deep gold rim; warming, fair, fruity nose, some cinnamon; fair fruit, quite rich palate, walnuts, but fiery edge. **Good.**

BONNIN

Le Logis de la Montagne, 16300 Challignac
tel: (33-5) 45 78 52 71
Visitors Monday–Saturday from 9.00am–6.00pm

*B*onnin has had vine-growers for four generations with 98.8 acres for both cognac and Pineau des Charentes. About 106,000 gallons of wine is made at the property at Challignac in the Fins Bois district.

Bonnin was awarded the gold medal at the 1993 Vinexpo and silver medal at the same competition in 1995. The VS is four years old, the VSOP 10 years, Napoléon 15 years, and XO 20 years. The Bonnin labels cover Logis de la Montagne, Vicomte de Castelbajac, Domaine de Fontanger, and Valcoeur.

Tasting Note

L. de la Montagne Réserve VSOP
(silver medal 1995 winner at challenge international du vin)
Mid-ocher hue; elegant, softish fruit on nose; palate suggests ice-cream soda, spirity finish, fair length. **Good to very good.**

DE LA
MONTAGNE
RÉSERVE

- RANGE -
THREE STAR
VS
VSOP
NAPOLÉON
XO

CAMUS

Le Grande Marque, 29 rue Marguerite de
Navarre, B.P. 19, 16101 Cognac
tel: (33-5) 45 32 28 28
Visitors from May–October, Monday–Friday 10.00AM–12 noon, 2.30–4.30PM

Camus was founded in 1863 by Jean Baptiste Camus and today is an independent company employing 280 and is the largest family-owned cognac house. Now the fifth generation, headed by Jean-Paul Camus, oversees the export of 94 percent of production to over 140 countries.

Just 8 percent of Camus's needs come from its own vineyards, providing 477,000 gallons. The 370.5 acres are at Château d'Uffaut (near Cognac) in the Grande Champagne (where the 49.4 acres are still harvested by hand) and at three properties in the Borderies district, which includes the Camus family house of Château du Plessis. About 2.7 million gallons wine—95 percent from Ugni Blanc grapes and the balance in Folle Blanche—are purchased additionally and distilled in four districts

JEAN-BAPTISTE CAMUS

CAMUS GRANDE VSOP

located in Grande Champagne, Borderies, Fins Bois, and Bons Bois. Camus prefers to distill on the *lees* for Grande and Petite Champagne and off the *lees* for Borderies.

Both Allier and Tronçais oak is used to mature the spirit, using some new wood each time. At La Nérolle distillery, Camus can store 1.85 million gallons.

A sister company of Camus, Compagnie des Grandes Eaux-de-Vie de France (CGEVF) has four cognac blends: Chabanneau, Planat, Staub, and Guillot. It also markets two brands of Pineau des Charentes (Plessis and St. Michel) and has interests in Calvados and non-cognac brandy. It is based at Logis de Brissac-l'Épine in Cherves Richemont.

- **RANGE** -

VS DE LUXE

GRAND VSOP

VSOP DE LUXE

NAPOLÉON VIEILLE RÉSERVE

XO SUPERIEUR

EXTRA

CUVÉE SPÉCIALE

JOSÉPHINE

SPECIAL RÉSERVE

EXTRAORDINAIRE

COGNAC
CAMUS
GRAND
V.S.O.P.
70 cl   40% vol.
16100 COGNAC - FRANCE

JOSÉPHINE POUR FEMME

CHÂTEAU DU PLESSIS, THE CAMUS FAMILY HOME.

LA NEROLLE DISTILLERY IN GRANDE CHAMPAGNE.

STORAGE CELLARS AT LA NEROLLE DISTILLERY.

Annually Camus sells about six million bottles split 20 percent Three Star, 52 percent VSOP and 28 percent Napoléon, XO, and Extra. It does not supply supermarkets under their own label. Camus enjoys substantial duty-free sales and good trade in Japan, the U.S., Hong Kong, Singapore, South Korea, Taiwan, Ukraine, Australia, Malaysia, and Russia.

Camus won gold medals at the 1968 Wine and Alcohol Fair, 1981 Igeho Spirit Competition, 1975 Mercury International Award Competition, and at the 1984, 1987, and 1989 U.K.-based International Wine and Spirit Competition.

Tasting Notes

JOSÉPHINE "POUR FEMME" (FOR WOMEN)

Mid-depth appearance; soft, delicate almond / vanilla fruit on nose; smooth, elegant, apricots on taste, nutty, very good length. **Very good.**

GRAND VSOP

Quite deep hue; delicate, stylish nose; softening, sweet fruity taste with fair length. **Good.**

VSOP DE LUXE

Mid-depth; violets on nose, quite appealing; honeyed fruit on palate but fiery final edge, mid-length. **Good.**

NAPOLÉON VIEILLE RÉSERVE

Mid-tawny hue; lovely, high-quality, fruity nose, prunes, elegant; soft fruit on palate, good length, slightly harsh finish. **Good to very good.**

NAPOLÉON EXTRA OLD

Mid-tawny appearance; hazel nuts, rather spirity nose; soft palate, showing vanilla oak, supple, mid-length. **Very good.**

XO SUPERIEUR

Mid-tawny hue; good fruit, some almonds on nose; quite stylish fruit on palate, mid-length. Light overall. **Good.**

CAMUS XO
SUPERIEUR

CCG

B.P. 10, 16101 COGNAC
TEL: (33-5) 45 82 32 10

*C*ompagnie Commerciale de Guyenne (CCG) is an independent family firm, created in 1978 by Michel Coste and employing 120 people. Its cognac activity results from the takeover of several small- and medium-sized firms: Bastier-Chagnaud, Brugerolle, Courant, Favraud, Foucauld, Meukow, Réau Richard, and Rouyer-Guillet. The Brugerolle company bottles Rouyer-Guillet, Meukow, and its own brands, various secondary labels, as well as acting as a brand distributor from its modern plant in Matha, 15.5 miles from Cognac. Its bottling capacity is 4,500 bottles per hour. CCG also handles Armagnac, non-cognac brandy, gin, vodka, and Scotch whisky.

In 1847, Jean Brugerolle, together with his nephew, Etienne, founded the firm, "Brugerolle Uncle & Nephew–Wine Merchants & Landlords," in Matha in the heart of the Fins Bois district. Etienne managed it from 1880 with his two children, Henri and Léopold. The latter greatly increased sales of Brugerolle, not only in France but in most European states and, from 1905, in the U.S.

In 1912, Léopold Brugerolle purchased Château de Bardon, near Matha. It used to be the monastery of the village of Thors but was probably destroyed during the French Revolution. The present property was built in the early-nineteenth century but still retains fifteenth-century moats and a seventeenth-century dovecot. Its vineyards are used for a Pineau des Charentes.

Léopold Brugerolle's great grandson, Claude, is now both vice president of CCG International and president of Brugerolle Cognac, living at Château de Bardon and managing the property. Brugerolle is noted for its XO, a blend of cognacs from the Grande and Petite Champagne districts.

Meukow, an old established brand, was purchased by CCG in 1978. Meukow was founded in 1862 by Auguste and Carl Meukow, two brothers and Siberian merchants who had come to Cognac for the Russian Czar. The countryside of Charente was so appealing that they decided to stay. Formerly well known in Leningrad and Moscow, Meukow is widely distributed in Scandinavia and the Far East.

A new range of high-quality cognacs has been launched for Meukow under the Feline label: a VSOP and XO in a beautiful bottle.

CCG purchases about 53,000 gallons wine which it distills at its Rouyer-Guillet plant in Saintes. Maturation is in both Limousin and Tronçais oak with casks up to 172 gallons capacity. They are kept for a maximum of 10 years.

- RANGE -

BRUGEROLLE XO
FINE CHAMPAGNE

MEUKOW VSOP
SUPÉRIEUR

MEUKOW XO

BRUGEROLLE
XO FINE
CHAMPAGNE

Tasting Notes

BRUGEROLLE XO FINE CHAMPAGNE

(PRESENTED IN AN ELEGANT DECANTER)

Deep tawny hue; almonds, softening, good fruit on nose; lovely fruity palate, smooth style and supple.
Very good.

MEUKOW VSOP SUPÉRIEUR

(BEAUTIFULLY PACKAGED IN AN ELEGANT OVAL BOTTLE, EMBOSSED WITH A CHEETAH)

Mid-tawny hue; rather spirity, fair fruit with coconut on nose; fiery fruit on palate, quite rich, mid-length. **Good.**

MEUKOW XO

(LOVELY PRESENTATION WITH AN EMBOSSED BOUNDING CHEETAH IN GOLD ACROSS THE BOTTLE)

Bright, mid-tawny core with wide, pale lemon rim; nutty, wood/vanilla overtones and cinnamon on nose; good, inviting fruit, soft style on palate, showing many layers, good length. **Very good to exceptional.**

MEUKOW
XO

CHABASSE

47 RUE ÉLYSÉE-LOUSTALOT, B.P. 10,
17412 ST. JEAN D'ANGÉLY
TEL: (33-5) 46 32 11 48
Visitors by appointment

habasse was founded in 1818 by Jean-Baptiste Chabasse, who was born in 1787 in Saint Jean d'Angély, north of Cognac in the Fins Bois district. Today the family tradition of blending fine cognac is continued by René-Luc Chabasse from the seventeenth-century manor house which lies in the heart of the town.

Only two districts are used for Chabasse: half Petite Champagne and the balance Fins Bois, purchased as spirit because the firm has no stills. Only Limousin oak is used, some of which is new from the Vicard cooperage and the balance is four to five years old.

BOWEN XO

Its main markets are Asia (Japan, South Korea, Hong Kong, Taiwan, China) and Europe (Spain, Belgium, Luxembourg, the Netherlands, Germany). The XO Imperial won the packaging award in the prestige section of the 1994 IFEC.

Chabasse has another brand, Bowen, which took its name from Elisabeth Bowen. She met René-Luc Chabasse's grandfather, Louis-Olivier Chabasse, on one of his travels to promote the family cognac. Bowen was running a farm on the east coast of India, near Madras. Louis-Olivier was so captivated by the lady that he prepared a special cognac that was particularly aromatic. For Bowen, one third each comes from Petite Champagne, Fins Bois, and Borderies respectively.

The VSOP in the Chabasse range accounts for 30 percent of sales; it is said to show the power of the fruity Fins Bois with the floral aromas of the Petite Champagne. Napoléon, which is 20 percent of

- RANGE -

CHABASSE VSOP

CHABASSE NAPOLÉON

CHABASSE XO

CHABASSE XO IMPÉRIAL

BOWEN VSOP

BOWEN NAPOLÉON

BOWEN XO

BOWEN EXTRA

CHABASSE XO IMPÉRIAL

sales, is reported to show distinct vanilla from the Limousin oak maturation with "aromas of cooked fruit, plums and pears, backed by an extremely pleasant and discreet touch of Port," according to René-Luc Chabasse.

The Chabasse XO is packed in a stylish oval bottle and accounts for half their sales. Chabasse waxes lyrical about it: "The characteristics of vintage Port melt into somewhat rounder aromas of dry fruit, such as hazelnut and walnut, after floral touches of iris and hyacinth which add a freshness to this harmonious blend."

The XO Impérial is given 50 years of aging, producing aromas of cigar boxes, dried leaves, and old roses with a hint of hazelnut and walnut, according to Chabasse; on the palate, he detects the spice of cinnamon, saffron, and ginger.

The Bowen range starts with a VSOP, which is a blend of Borderies, Fins Bois, and Petite Champagne. Napoléon is described by Chabasse as "a round and harmonious cognac, backed by subtle aromas of wild violets and jasmine, typical of the fine Borderies; its fine mahogany color is deeper and softer."

The XO in the Bowen range is distilled on the *lees*. The Extra won the 1995 IFEC packaging award. It is reported to have aromas

reminiscent of cashew nuts and the discreet tang of preserved citrus fruit, together with the typical Charentais *rancio* quality.

Tasting Notes

BOWEN XO

Mid-tawny core with mid-ocher rim appearance; very soft nose, floral (violets from the Borderies and iris and wisteria from Petite Champagne); palate shows tangy tangerine fruit with walnut tones, a slightly harsh edge, mid-length. **Fair to good.**

DOMINIQUE CHAINIER et Fils

LA BARDE FAGNOUSE, 17520 ARTHENAC
TEL: (33-5) 46 49 12 85
Visitors by appointment

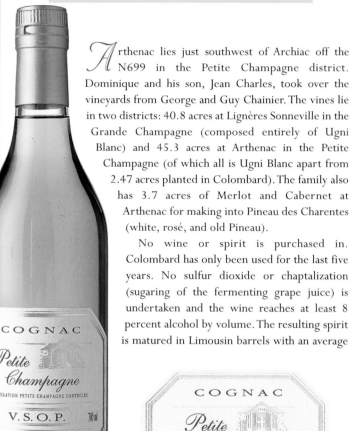

Arthenac lies just southwest of Archiac off the N699 in the Petite Champagne district. Dominique and his son, Jean Charles, took over the vineyards from George and Guy Chainier. The vines lie in two districts: 40.8 acres at Lignères Sonneville in the Grande Champagne (composed entirely of Ugni Blanc) and 45.3 acres at Arthenac in the Petite Champagne (of which all is Ugni Blanc apart from 2.47 acres planted in Colombard). The family also has 3.7 acres of Merlot and Cabernet at Arthenac for making into Pineau des Charentes (white, rosé, and old Pineau).

No wine or spirit is purchased in. Colombard has only been used for the last five years. No sulfur dioxide or chaptalization (sugaring of the fermenting grape juice) is undertaken and the wine reaches at least 8 percent alcohol by volume. The resulting spirit is matured in Limousin barrels with an average

VSOP PETITE CHAMPAGNE

CARTE BLANCHE

VS

VSOP

VIEILLE RÉSERVE

TRÈS VIEILLE
RÉSERVE

RÉSERVE DU
CHAIGNE

age of seven years, including some new ones introduced each year. Their cooper, M. Allary, is based in Archiac.

The spirit is initially matured at full 70 percent strength and reduced between two and five years of age. The annual 10,000 bottles are sold in Germany, Denmark, Belgium, and France.

Tasting Notes

VSOP PETITE CHAMPAGNE

Very light appearance; gentle coconut and vanilla nose; softening fruit with apricots, mid-length on palate. **Good.**

GRANDE CHAMPAGNE RÉSERVE DU CHAIGNE

Mid-ocher hue; very stylish nose with soft, fruity tones; elegant fruit with long length on palate. ***Very good.***

GRANDE CHAMPAGNE RÉSERVE DU CHAIGNE

COURVOISIER

2 PLACE DU CHÂTEAU, 16200 JARNAC
TEL: (33-5) 45 35 56 16/05 45 35 55 87
*Visitors (free guided tours) from October 1–May 31 between 9.30–11.00AM
and from June 1–September 30 between 9.30AM–5.00PM*

*I*n the early nineteenth century, Emmanuel Courvoisier visited Paris and met Louis Gallois, a successful wine and spirit merchant. They formed a partnership and succeeded in supplying the Imperial court. Napoléon visited their warehouses in Bercy in 1811, and it is known that their cognac was supplied on his campaigns. Furthermore, Courvoisier was placed on board the ship, HMS *Northumberland*, which took Napoléon to exile on St. Helena and it became known as "the brandy of Napoléon." Today the silhouette of Napoléon appears on all Courvoisier's labels.

In 1835, the sons of the founders merged their businesses and established their headquarters in Jarnac. By 1869, it was official supplier to the court of Napoléon III. The firm was acquired by Guy and George Simon (members of an English family of French origin) in 1909. Innovative marketing followed, including the introduction of a frosted bottled in 1960. In 1964, Courvoisier was sold to Hiram Walker which in turn was purchased in 1987 by Allied-Lyons, known since 1994 as Allied-Domecq (following the acquisition of Pedro Domecq). Today it employs some 300 staff.

COURVOISIER VSOP

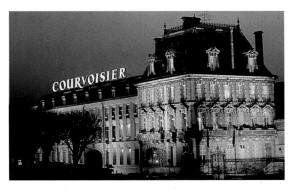

COURVOISIER'S HEADQUARTERS AT CHÂTEAUNEUF NEAR JARNAC.

Courvoisier today is one of the leading companies in Cognac, shipping 1.1 million bottles (13 percent of the market). It is sold in 160 countries, principally in the U.S., U.K., duty-free, Japan, Hong Kong, Italy, and France. It is the leading supplier or co-leader in 46 markets.

It owns no vineyards but has three-year rolling contracts with 1,200 vine growers who supply wine, raw spirit, and occasionally aged cognac. This means the firm has about 24,700 acres under contract, located in the top four districts (Grande and Petite Champagne, Borderies, and Fins Bois). The Ugni Blanc grape accounts for 98 percent.

Courvoisier owns two distilleries at Chateauneuf, near Jarnac. It also has contracts with nine *bouilleurs de profession* (distillers) and purchases from 200 *bouilleurs de cru*. Courvoisier use less than 1 percent caramel in the VS and VSOP styles to ensure uniformity of color. No preheating in a *chauffe-vin* is undertaken. It depends on the year whether distillation is on or off the *lees* (such as in 1996 when it was on the *lees* for more complexity) but usually not for Fins Bois as this is a short-term aging spirit. No *boisé* is used, because Courvoisier prefers a lighter style, taking natural color from the new wood.

- RANGE -

VS/THREE STAR
(4–8 YEARS OLD)

VSOP
(8–12 YEARS OLD)

VSOP EXCLUSIF
(FOR ASIAN MARKET)

FCN EXCLUSIF FINE
CHAMPAGNE

NAPOLÉON
(15–25 YEARS OLD)

XO IMPERIAL
(BLEND CONTAINING
COGNACS UP TO
34 YEARS OLD)

INITIALE EXTRA
(OVER 50 YEARS OLD)

COLLECTION ERTÉ
(12,000 DECANTERS
PER DESIGN
RELEASED)

For aging, most of its wood originates in the forests in central France, because it prefers a smaller grain. The oak trees are personally selected by the master blender and dried naturally for three years prior to use. The new spirit spends 6–24 months in new barrels, depending on the final quality sought. The cognac is then transferred into old casks for the rest of its maturation. About 2,000 new barrels are purchased annually, mostly from three different cooperages. It maintains an impressive warehouse outside Jarnac where barrels are stacked vertically four high for three to four years.

The cognac is kept for three months at full still strength (70 percent volume) and then reduced to 60 percent. Cognac intended for VS is further reduced after about one year to 55 percent but not for five to seven years for the other styles. Cane sugar in syrup form may be added just prior to bottling.

The range is sold at 40 percent volume alcohol. High stock holdings are maintained, equivalent to 86 million bottles, ensuring a consistency of style from year to year.

Many awards over the years have been secured including Prestige de la France (1983), best XO in the world (1986 in The International Wine & Spirit Competition), and the 1994 Cyril Ray Trophy for the XO Imperial as the finest Cognac.

Courvoisier also owns the house of Salignac, which sells principally on the North American market.

In addition to cognac, the company has a plant supplying the local wine under the designation of Vin de Pays Charentais. This is both bottled for the U.K. market and supplied in bulk to Germany as a base for sparkling wine.

Located by the river Charente, Courvoisier has a splendid museum of Napoleonic memorabilia. The wardrobe includes his famous hat as well as overcoat, waistcoat, and even lock of hair. Visitors can follow the various stages of production from vine cultivation to distillation, barrel-making, and blending. The oldest bottle held in its reserve or, "paradis," dates from 1789, and fine old stocks can be seen held in glass demijohns.

Art and cognac combine in Courvoisier's commission of designs by the French Art-Deco artist, Erté, which started in 1988. The first design, entitled "Vigne" (vine), was limited to 12,000 bottles—as each of the next six limited editions were—and included 1892 Grande Champagne. Erté was given artistic freedom both with the design of the bottle and its decoration. On the reverse of the bottle, the gold vine leaf symbolizes the precious quality of the grapes that went into this rare blend. Each bottle is individually treated over a month, involving silk-screening of 18 different colors and four separate kiln firings. Twenty-four carat gold is hand-painted onto the bottle. The subjects are Vine, Harvest, Distillation, Aging, Tasting, The Spirit of Cognac, The Angels' Share, and "Inedit" (a portrait of a nude woman), which was limited to 4,000 bottles.

A STUNNING EXAMPLE OF A BOTTLE FROM COLLECTION ERTÉ, SO NAMED AFTER THE FRENCH ARTIST WHO DESIGNED THE BOTTLES.

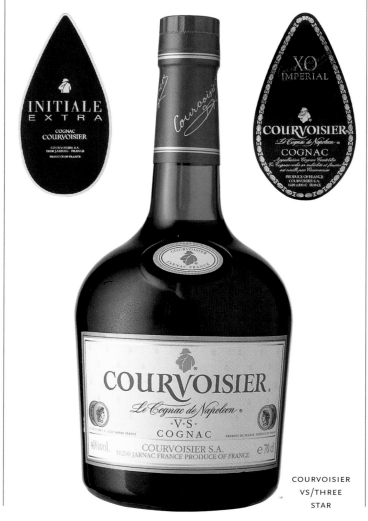

COURVOISIER VS/THREE STAR

Tasting Notes

VS/THREE STAR
(IN DISTINCTIVE JOSÉPHINE BOTTLE, INTRODUCED IN 1950)

Mainly Fins Bois, mellowed with Petite Champagne: warm, rather heavy fruit. **Fair.**

VSOP FINE CHAMPAGNE
(FROSTED BOTTLE)

Warm, fair fruit; more elegant than the VS. **Fair to good.**

NAPEOLÉON FINE CHAMPAGNE
(FROSTED BOTTLE)

Showing smoky fruit, reminiscent of box of cigars; warming fruit. **Good.**

XO IMPERIAL

Much finer, stylish; elegant fruit with hint of cigar box. The Grande and Petite Champagnes give depth and elegance, while the 25-year-old Borderies impart cinnamon and fennel aromas. **Very good.**

INITIALE EXTRA

Elegant and delicate, using Grande Champagne and old Borderies with a minimum 50-year age; hint of violets and spice. **Very good.**

COLLECTION ERTÉ
(LIMITED AND NUMBERED DESIGNS BY ERTÉ)

Grande Champagne showing smoky fruit, richer than Initiale; it includes some 1892. **Very good.**

COURVOISIER
XO IMPERIAL

CROIZET

B.P. 3, 16720 St. Même-les-Carrières
tel: (33-5) 45 81 90 11
Visitors by appointment

*T*he Croizet family became known for its large vineyard holding in the Grande Champagne district in the seventeenth century. In 1805, Léon Croizet founded the company which is based at St. Même-les-Carrières (between Jarnac and Châteauneuf-sur-Charente). He was awarded the Légion d'Honneur medal for his research into combating the aphid *phylloxera* and applying the principle of grafting onto American rootstocks.

Croizet has several properties in the Grande Champagne: Domaine de Flaville (88.9 acres), Maine Androux (44.6 acres), Domaine des Couronnes de Douvesse (88.9 acres), and Château de l'Epine (148.2 acres). Domaine de Flaville was once a hunting lodge which belonged to the Duke of Montmorency Bouteville, who lived in the castle nearby.

CROIZET XO

- 82 -

Together the family estates cover over 1.8 million square yards of vineyard, distilleries, warehouses, and offices. Their vineyards account for about 430,000 vines, yielding 265,000 –424,000 gallons. Croizet purchase about 265,000 gallons wine and 79,500 gallons immature cognac. Their total makes 70 percent Grande Champagne, 15 percent Petite Champagne and 15 percent from the Fins Bois and Bons Bois districts.

Aging is in Limousin oak, some in new barrels but most over 15 years old. Their reserve stock includes rare pre-*phylloxera* cognac which was given as a dowry in 1892 on the marriage of Miss Croizet to Mr. J. Eymard. In the past, much of the stock was

- **RANGE** -

CROIZET VS

CARRIÈRE VS

DORLAN VS

BOYARD VS

MATTE VS

CROIZET VSOP

CROIZET NAPOLÉON

CROIZET XO

CROIZET RÉSERVE PARTICULIÈRE

aged in underground cellars up to 164 feet deep, which had been quarried out for stone used in buildings in the region; part of the village name "Carrières" means quarries.

Awards over the years have included gold medals at the Paris Exhibition in 1878, in Amsterdam, Moscow (1891), and Leipzig (1974). Croizet is proudest of its older and rarer cognacs, such as the 15-year-old XO. Now in its seventh generation, this family cognac firm has shown such assiduous record-keeping that it has been permitted to sell some cognacs as single vintages. Many leading chefs have chosen its cognacs, including Troisgros, la Tour d'Argent, and Vergé. They bottle some under "own label," such as "Vicomte de Bressiac." Sales are particularly strong in the Far East (Japan, Hong Kong, China, Taiwan, and Korea).

Tasting Notes

CROIZET XO "AGE INCONNU"
(AGE UNKNOWN — PRESENTED IN STYLISH OVAL DECANTER)

Mid-tawny core with tight ocher rim; warm, fruity nose, quite stylish, hazel-nut tones; supple attractive fruit, many layers, quite rich, mid-length but final fiery edge.
Good to very good.

A. de LUZE

B.P. 37, 16102 Cognac
tel: (33-5) 57 97 07 20
Visitors by appointment

A. de Luze was founded in 1820 by Alfred de Luze in Bordeaux to supply cognac to his brother, Louis-Philippe, for his firm in New York. By 1824, de Luze was trading in fine wine and mature cognac. Agencies were soon established in England, the Indies, and Russia. During Napoléon III's era, the emblem of Baron de Luze was seen across the royal courts of Europe.

Alfred de Luze died in 1880 and was succeeded by his grandson who started exporting to Egypt and the Dutch Indies. In 1927, they were appointed suppliers to the Danish crown. The company was purchased by Rémy Martin in 1980 and is now part of the Rémy Cointreau group.

De Luze makes about 79,500 gallons cognac, entirely from Ugni Blanc grapes. The source is 90 percent Fins Bois and

- **RANGE** -

THREE STAR

VSOP

NAPOLÉON

XO

GRAND COGNAC
NAPOLÉON

10 percent Bons Bois/Bois Ordinaires. Only Limousin oak is used, with no new barrels; the average age is 15 years, and the casks are obtained from Seguin Moreau.

The main market is Scandinavia, but there are sales throughout Europe and the Far East, including an own label to such groups as Aldi (Germany) and Tesco (U.K.). About 1 million bottles are sold of VS/Three Star, 145,000 bottles VSOP, and 28,500 QSS.

The Napoléon is packed in an attractive squat, fluted decanter and other qualities use such shapes as an Eiffel Tower and even the Statue of Liberty.

THREE STAR

VSOP

Tasting Notes

THREE STAR

Quite dark hue, almondy fruit on nose; initially quite rich and smooth on palate but a harsh final taste. **Fair.**

VSOP

Mid-tawny hue; pineapple aroma; a little harsh on palate and without good balance but fair length. **Fair to good.**

GRAND COGNAC NAPOLÉON

Mid- to deep tawny hue; prune and hazle nuts on nose; palate shows softening, quite rich good fruit but slightly fiery finish. **Good.**

DE LUZE XO GRANDE
(LIMITED AND NUMBERED PRESENTED IN ATTRACTIVE SQUARE-SHAPED DECANTER)

Mid-tawny core with long, pale ocher rim; nose shows soft, light fruit with appealing vanilla and hazel nuts; warming, fruity palate with soft apricot tones, inviting, mid-length. **Very good.**

XO
GRANDE

GASTON de LAGRANGE

Château de Cognac, B.P. 3, 16101 Cognac
TEL: (33-5) 45 36 88 88
No visitors

*G*aston de Lagrange was established in 1961 by the vermouth giants, Martini & Rossi. It is named after a French aristocrat, Comte Gaston de Lagrange. No vineyards are owned but about 53,000 gallons immature cognac are purchased, mainly from the Ugni Blanc grape.

The spirit is matured at 55–65 percent alcohol and reduced gradually. Only 5 percent new casks are used. Oak from the Limousin forest in central France are used by three cooperages for its casks. Sales in bottle are 375,000 for VS, 55,000 for VSOP, and 27,000 for the two XOs, all at 40 percent.

Four districts (Grande and Petite Champagne, Borderies, and Fins Bois) are used for the range, apart from Grande Champagne for the superior XO which carries the district name.

- **RANGE** -

VS

VSOP

XO

XO Grande
Champagne

DE LAGRANGE VS

The cellar master considers that the balance between the four districts is ideal for the first three cognacs, combining the delicate yet subtle flavors of the Grande and Petite Champagne with the floral character of the Borderies and fruit of the Fins Bois. The XO Grande Champagne has brandy up to 35 years old.

Gaston de Lagrange is exported to over 50 countries. The main markets are France, Belgium, Canada, the U.S., and those in the Far East. It has not entered competitions recently. The house considers its cognac "the best value for money for consumers."

Tasting Notes

VS

Light straw appearance; soft, almonds on nose; softening fruit, quite stylish taste, mid-length, slightly fiery end.
Good.

VSOP

Mid-straw hue; heavy fruit with almonds; raisiny young walnuts on taste, slightly bitter finish, mid-length.
Fair to good.

DE LAGRANGE VSOP

L. de SALIGNAC

2 place du Château, 16200 Jarnac
tel: (33-5) 45 35 55 55

*Visitors May–October Monday–Sunday including bank holidays
9.30am–4.45pm. Rest of the year by appointment. Tour includes a visit to the
museum and warehouse where cognac is matured. Visitors receive a brochure
and a 3cl bottle of cognac*

*S*alignac is a name of Roman origin, designating the property of a Roman farmer who settled in the Cognac region after Caesar's conquest of Gaul. Literally, Salgnac means "Salus' estate" and probably refers to the first settler. The family can be traced back to the sixteenth century and its coat of arms is frequently found on many official documents.

Antoine de Salignac, who was born in 1753, started trading in cognac with a business associate in 1802 and headed the firm—known as Salignac & Fils—from 1809, in association with his son, Pierre-Antoine. The latter effectively developed a cooperative between vine-growers and distillers to ensure continuity of supply. He was also innovative in classifying cognac according to

- RANGE -

VS Three Star

VSOP

Napoléon Fine
Champagne

XO

L. DE SALIGNAC VSOP

district and maturation, the first major step towards ensuring a quality reputation for the spirit.

These initiatives brought success to the firm which by 1870 became the third largest cognac house. A descendant, Louis, changed the company name in 1898 to Louis de Salignac. The firm merged with Henry Roy in 1924, and the business was acquired by Hiram Walker in 1974, subsequently becoming part of Allied Domecq and a subsidiary of Courvoisier. Over the years, Salignac has had many appreciative customers including Winston Churchill, Harry Truman, and Konrad Adenauer.

Tasting Notes

L. DE SALIGNAC VS

Rich, amber core with watery lemon rim; fiery, coarse, fruity nose; fiery, rough fruit on palate, sultanas, mid-length. **Fair.**

L. DE SALIGNAC VSOP

Light appearance — mid-straw; nose shows vanilla, fruit but lacks style; palate of coarse fruit, fiery, mid-length. **Fair.**

DEAU

SOCIÉTÉ DES VINS & SPIRITUEUX, DOMAINE DU
CHAILLAUD, 17260 ST. ANDRÉ DE LIDON
TEL: (33-5) 46 90 08 10
Visitors (daily guided tours) 9.30AM–5.30PM

*D*eau can trace its history back to Louys Deau, who became a vine-grower under Louis XIV in the Corme Royal parish in the Saintonge district of Cognac. Prior to the 1789 Revolution, the family became *bouilleurs de cru*. The current generation is represented by Jean-Marie Deau, who took over in 1972 at the age of just 21 years. For many years, the firm sold cognac, local wine, and Pineau des Charentes in bulk, but in 1994 introduced its own range in bottle.

- RANGE -

DEAU VS

DEAU VSOP

DEAU NAPOLÉON
EXTRA OLD

DEAU XO

DEAU EXTRA

J.M. DEAU VSOP

J.M. DEAU XO
NO. 8

J.M. DEAU EXTRA
ETERNITÉ

DEAU VSOP

Its own vineyards around Château de Longchamp extend to over 247 acres, partly owned by the Deau family and the balance by Jean-Marie Deau's spouse's family. They lie in the Borderies, Fins Bois, and Bons Bois districts, and account for 20–30 percent of their needs, supplying 318,000 gallons. In addition, 13,250–26,500 gallons immature spirit is purchased from all six Cognac districts.

Deau's two vineyards are planted with Ugni Blanc (155.6 acres), Colombard (24.7 acres), Folle Blanche (17.3 acres), Montils (6.2 acres) for cognac and with four grapes for wine and Pineau des Charentes: Merlot (11.1 acres), Cabernet (8.65 acres), Sauvignon Blanc (18.5 acres), Chardonnay (12.4 acres).

The cellars were modernized in 1991 to ensure better control of the fermentation, separation of the different grape varieties, and blending of the cognacs. Distillation is no longer on site. Limousin oak with an average

DEAU XO

age of 30 years is used for the casks. New wood is purchased each year for the freshly distilled cognac.

In bottles, VS accounts for 40,000, VSOP for 30,000, Napoléon for 30,000, XO for 20,000, and Extra for 5,000. Sales are to the Leclerc supermarkets in France and to Germany, Belgium, and the U.K. (including the Ritz in London). Competitions are not entered into.

St. André de Lidon lies east of Cozes (in the southwest part of Bons Bois).

NAPOLÉON
EXTRA OLD

Magnificent gardens are maintained at Domaine du Chaillaud, including 600 species of trees, shrubs, perennials, and roses, together with a nineteenth-century greenhouse. The guided tours include visiting the cellars, tasting room (where cognac from five to 100 years as well as Pineau des Charentes can be tasted), and an audio-visual presentation. Colette Deau advises to allow three hours for a full visit, including the 4.9 acres of garden.

Deau's VS has an average of five years; they say it "is superior to other cognacs" and advise that if served over ice or accompanied with tonic water, it produces complex aromas. The VSOP is 6–8 years, Napoléon Extra Vieux 12–15 years, XO 20 years, and Extra over half a century old. At the 1995 Vinexpo, a luxury range was launched with the packaging designed by Pierre Dinand, noted for his fragrance designs for Paco Rabanne, Van Cleef, and Calvin Klein.

Tasting Notes

VS

Mid-straw hue; prunes and figs on nose; warm, soft fruit on palate with good length; some vanilla. **Good.**

VSOP

Quite deep straw appearance; sweet, elegant, fruity nose, quite mellow; fair fruit and length on taste but with rather a harsh fiery edge. **Fair to good.**

NAPOLÉON EXTRA OLD

Pale tawny hue; not unified on nose, pineapple tones; unripe fruit, syrupy palate with bitter finish. **Fair.**

DELAMAIN

7 RUE J & R DELAMAIN, B.P. 16, 16200 JARNAC
TEL: (33-5) 45 81 08 24
Visitors by appointment all year (except August 1–21 and Christmas)
from Monday–Thursday 9.00AM–4.00PM, Friday mornings

The smallest of the great cognac houses, the Delamains have contributed to many fields. Nicholas Delamain accompanied Henrietta Maria, Charles I's bride, to London in 1625 as her chef-de-suite and was knighted 14 years later. He settled in Ireland, becoming a noted Protestant landowner. Another scion of the family, Henry Delamain, became a potter in Dublin; the Irish Parliament granted him £100 in recognition of him being the first to use coal to fire Delftware, an event commemorated in recent years on a series of Irish postage stamps.

James Delamain, Henry's nephew, son of the Constable of Dublin Castle, returned to the family's roots in the Cognac region in 1759 and entered the brandy trade. Three years later, he became a partner with his father-in-law, Isaac Ranson, in a Jarnac firm that had been exporting cognac to Holland and Ireland. After the upheavals of the Revolution and Empire, the 1815 Restoration marked the renaissance of the cognac trade. With his Roullet cousins, James's grandson–Henry Delamain–founded the House of Roullet and Delamain in 1824. It traded under this name for four generations. In 1920, the Delamain family was left as sole owner and changed the company name to Delamain & Co.

DELAMAIN
1960 GRANDE
CHAMPAGNE

The Delamain directors have contributed to many aspects of life. Jacques was a pioneer of modern ornithology and nature studies, writing several books on bird life, one of which won a prize from the Académie Française. Jean, his son, was a leading botanist and discovered several European wild orchids. Maurice, one of his brothers, founded the Parisian publishing house of Stock, Delamain & Boutelleau, which introduced many noted Anglo-Saxon authors—such as Thomas Wolfe, Pearl Buck, and Robert Penn Warren—to French readers. Another brother, Robert, wrote the definitive background of the region, *L'Histoire du Cognac*, in 1935.

Today, Delamain is still very much a family concern: Alain Braastad, whose mother is a Delamain, runs the firm with Patrick Peyrelongue, whose grandmother was a Delamain.

- RANGE -

PALE & DRY GRANDE CHAMPAGNE

VESPER GRANDE CHAMPAGNE

TRÈS VÉNÉRABLE GRANDE CHAMPAGNE

TRÈS VIEILLE RÉSERVE DE LA FAMILLE GRANDE CHAMPAGNE

VINTAGE 1949, 1960, 1963, 1968

EARLY LANDED

Despite the imposing presence of an old pot still in their warehouse, the Delamains do not distill, neither do they own vineyards or ferment any wine. They are *négociants*—purchasing spirit at 10–15 years of age, maturing, blending, and bottling. All the stock originates in the Grande Champagne district, the "premier cru" (or first growth) of cognac.

ALAIN BRAASTED-DELAMAIN, PATRICK PEYRELONGUE, AND CHARLES BRAASTED-DELAMAIN.

AN OLD POT STILL IN THE DELAMAIN WAREHOUSE.

No new wood is used; instead seasoned barrels of at least six years, both Limousin and Tronçais, are employed. The Delamains maintain that during the long aging process a new cask would impart too tannic and woody an element. They do not operate on a contract basis, preferring instead to purchase after careful preliminary tastings from *bouilleurs de cru*.

The cognac is matured at whatever strength it has naturally reached when the Delamains buy it. The blending is undertaken at well above the final sales strength; for example, Pale & Dry, the youngest blend, although enjoying an average age of 25 years, is blended around 50 percent alcohol by volume. Another of their distinguishing differences from other houses is the way in which the eventual reduction is undertaken. Instead of adding distilled water alone, which Alain Braastad-Delamain maintains would "destroy the delicacy and balance," very old weak cognac together with distilled water, forming a mix of 15 percent alcohol (known as "vieilles faibles"), is gradually added over a period of 24 months.

When purchasing, Delamain prefers the spirit distilled on the *lees* to ensure more fruit and esters come through, but they watch for an excess. No sugar or syrup is added but caramel occasionally is to ensure consistency of color.

The source of Delamain Cognac, the Grande Champagne, has the highest concentration of vineyards and represents about 15 percent of the appellation. Delamain searches for cognacs that show delicacy and richness with subtle, clean aromas. It would be impossible for Delamain to mature all its stock from start to finish on its present site.

Grower-distillers prefer to hold on to some of their finest brandies in order to sell them nearing maturity at the highest price—and to provide a hedge against hard times. This is where Delamain's skills as a *négociant* come in.

The individual craftsmanship continues even at the stage of bottling. Bottles are washed and rinsed with cognac before filling and are then individually checked, hand-labeled, and sealed with gilt netting, as in the early days before capsules were applied.

Lightness, both in hue and style, is the hallmark of Delamain cognac. It is a reminder of the extraordinary diaphanous sky which sets the scene not only for the rolling Charentais landscape but also for the rows of vines set amid the many Romanesque churches and chapels. Yet in the glass, this lightness belies the breadth, structure, and lively style of a crafted Delamain cognac.

The Pale & Dry was developed in the 1920s and is the house's main line, accounting for 80 percent of sales. It takes the name "pale" because it is much lighter than other cognacs of comparable age (22–28 years), owing to maturation in old casks; the term "dry" refers to the fact that it has only its natural sweetness. Vesper is an older blend, created in the 1950s, with a more classic character. On average the brandies that form the blend are ten years older than those used

PALE AND DRY GRANDE CHAMPAGNE

for Pale & Dry. It is matured near to the Charente river in old cellars which are more humid than dry.

The oldest cognac in Delamain's standard range is Très Vénérable, averaging 50 years. Each constituent cognac is matured separately accord-ing to its origin and actual year of distillation prior to blending at 48 per-cent alcohol. The most limited edition, Réserve de la Famille, consists of very old brandy whose quality and distinction has been judged as so exceptional that it can be offered unblended. The current source is a cognac distilled before World War II by a master *bouilleur de cru* at his property near St. Preuil in the heart of the Grande Champagne. It was aged in wood for 55–60 years, then transferred to glass demijohns and preserved at its natural strength of 43 percent alcohol. The label has been specially printed on pure hand-made hemp paper at the Moulin du Verger near Angoulême.

Occasionally, Delamain releases a single vintage cognac. This might either be an "early landed" (for aging in England or Scotland) or when mature from Jarnac. They are one of the few cognac *négoçiants* to have been authorized to mature and sell such single vintages, a ruling

DELAMAIN'S AGING CELLARS.

introduced in 1988. Currently, Delamain offers a 1960 vintage which was purchased from a grower-distiller in Verrières near Segonzac; designed for the true connoisseur, it is rare and shows great purity of character. It is also possible to find the single vintages of 1949 and 1963, whereas "early landed" is usually shipped within 24 months of the distillation and typically not bottled until it has matured for 21 years in wood.

The quality of a cognac is determined by four factors, according to Alain Braastad-Delamain, each in equal parts: the distilled brandy before maturation, humidity of the cellars in which the aging takes place, skill of the blender, and time (i.e. the development of the cognac in cask). This quiet and persuasive diplomat for cognac says his house "offers the best price/quality ratio of practically any cognac on the market." This is a view echoed not only by the top hotels but in highly respected restaurants and by spirit retailers of note. As *Le Livre du Cognac* expressed it, "The Delamain family is to cognac what Rembrandt is to painting."

Tasting Notes

PALE & DRY GRANDE CHAMPAGNE

Delicate, slightly floral nose, many layered; mellow roundness on palate with fair fruit and balanced acidity.
Good to very good.

VESPER GRANDE CHAMPAGNE

(Named after the sixth canonical hour celebrated each late afternoon in song "to reflect its richness and the worshipful sense it imparts," according to Delamain); fuller and richer than the Pale & Dry on the nose with good depth and vanilla/rancio characteristics; full, rich, softening fruit on taste with long finish, showing good balance.
Very good to exceptional.

TRÈS VÉNÉRABLE GRANDE CHAMPAGNE

Paler than Vesper; both floral and spicy aromas with honeyed raisons, mellow and fruity; complex soft fruity palate, many layers, mid-length, slightly spirity finish.
Very good.

TRÈS VIEILLE RÉSERVE DE LA FAMILLE GRANDE CHAMPAGNE
(FORTY-THREE PERCENT ALCOHOL BY VOLUME. NUMBERED BOTTLES)

Quite woody nose with many layers of fruit; softening fruit on palate showing complex vanilla tones, mid-length: a memorable glass, reflecting the cognac's age and depth.
Very good to exceptional.

DOMPIERRE

DOMAINE DE FONTSÈCHE, 17610 DOMPIERRE SUR
CHARENTE
TEL: (33-5) 45 81 08 31
Visitors welcome

The vineyard for Domaine de Fontsèche is planted entirely with Ugni Blanc grapes and lies between the towns of Cognac and Saintes: 37 acres in the Borderies district and 61.8 acres in Fins Bois. This results in about 106,000 gallons. All the production is from their own estate with no wine or immature spirit purchased in.

Distillation takes place in the two pot stills, each of 663 gallons capacity, at the Domaine. The cognac is matured half in Allier oak and the balance in Tronçais, purchased from the Seguin Moreau and Vicard cooperages. It is gradually reduced in alcoholic strength from 70 to 40 percent.

Under the J. Bancel label, VSOP accounts for 80 percent of production with XO for the balance. The spirit is aged for at least four years and is then blended with Grande and Petite Champagne cognacs.

The Domaine houses a museum on cognac history, and the estate manager explains about the production methods used.

- RANGE -

VSOP
XO

Tasting Note

J. BANCEL VSOP

Bright mid tawny core with pale lemon rim; nose of subdued apricots; fair fruit, woody edge on palate; short length. **Fair to good.**

J BANCEL VSOP

A. E. DOR

4 RUE JACQUES MOREAU, 16200 JARNAC
TEL: (33-5) 545 36 88 68
Visitors welcome; groups by appointment

*D*or was established in 1858 by Amédée-Edouard Dor. From an old cognac family, Dor built up a reputation for fine mature cognacs—a tradition which has continued to the present generation, led by Jacques Riuère.

Around 24.7 acres are owned in Grande Champagne, Petite Champagne, and a small plot in the Fins Bois. Some 197.6 acres are under contract: 65 percent in Grande and Petite Champagne with the balance in Borderies, Fins Bois, and Bon Bois.

- **RANGE** -

SÉLÉCTION

RARE FINE CHAMPAGNE VSOP

NAPOLÉON

VIEILLE FINE CHAMPAGNE XO

GRANDE CHAMPAGNE
RÉSERVE NO. 6

RÉSERVE NO. 7

RÉSERVE NO. 8

RÉSERVE NO. 9

RÉSERVE NO. 10

RÉSERVE NO. 11

VIEILLE RÉSERVE NO. 6

Tasting Notes

SÉLECTION

Mid-straw core with wide, pale lemon rim; nose shows lightish fruit, fiery, reflecting largely youthful fins bois; slightly coarse palate, with harsh fiery fruit. **Disappointing.**

RARE FINE CHAMPAGNE

Mid-straw core with pale lemon rim appearance; nose shows slightly fiery fruit—apricots, quite warm; palate quite rich, heavy fruit; mid length. **Fair.**

NAPOLÉON

Deep gold core with wide pale lemon rim; delicate floral fruit on nose; supple, quite rich fruity taste with fiery edge. **Fair to good.**

XO

Deep gold core with wide pale ocher rim; quite rich nose, good supple fruit, almonds, many layers; rich fruity palate but rather fiery. **Fair to good.**

NO. 11 GRANDE CHAMPAGNE

Deep gold core with wide pale lemon rim; good fruity "rancio" with soft style on nose; palate shows good inviting fruit, supple, mid length. **Very good.**

The distillery is at Châteauneuf-sur-Charente in the Petite Champagne district (a small town equidistant between Cognac and Angoulême) with the wines off the *lees*. A *chauffe-vin* for pre-heating the wine is used.

The distinguishing feature of Dor is the special exemption gained in 1951 by Noël Denieul (who led the house from 1922–1971) in being the first firm authorized to sell cognac at less than 40 percent alcohol. This requirement has been made in the 1946 decree but Dor successfully argued that part of its stock had naturally fallen below this strength. Accordingly, they were able to continue selling it. Very old cognacs are moved from cask into glass demijohns. Dor says that most very old stocks are found to be "flat" in that they have lost their aroma and vigor but are often used to improve younger cognacs in a blend.

Dor is regularly available in leading hotels and restaurants, including the Everest Room and Park Hyatt (Chicago), Postrio and Stars (San Francisco), Red Sage (Washington), La Masia (Barcelona), Hiramatsu (Tokyo), Bath Spa (Bath, England), Middlethorpe Hall (York, England), and One Devonshire Gardens (Glasgow).

DUBOIGALANT

CHEZ GALLAND, 17520 ST. MARTIAL SUR NÉ
TEL: (33-5) 46 49 53 31
Visitors Monday—Friday by appointment

*D*uboigalant is a family company run by Jean Jacques Trijol, the fifth generation of vineyard owners and distillers who established their trade in 1859.

Only Grande Champagne grapes are used for Duboigalant (unlike the associate company, Trijol). Ugni Blanc accounts for 90 percent and the balance comes from Folle Blanche and Colombard. The family vineyard covers 49.4 acres and lies in the Salles d'Angles parish, west of Segonzac.

The distillery at St. Martial sur Né is equipped with 18 Charente pot stills. Only oak from Limousin is used. Elégance is matured initially at 65 percent, VSOP at 58 percent and XO at 47 percent.

Elégance is a new line, a blend of 4- and 12-year-old cognacs. The VSOP sells about 10,000 bottles, XO 5,000 bottles (in a magnificent oval decanter with gold lettering), and the Très Rare 1,000 bottles. Wire mesh covers the bottles to make them visually appealing. Major sales are to Germany, France, the U.K., Belgium, Luxembourg, Switzerland, Sweden, Finland, Taiwan, and Florida. Duboigalant emphasizes that it markets "only batches with outstanding quality (based on) extremely vigorous selection." This naturally limits production. No *boisé*, sugar or syrup solution is used. The alcoholic strength is reduced by adding distilled water.

DUBOIGALANT TRÈS RARE GRANDE CHAMPAGNE

Tasting Notes

VSOP GRANDE CHAMPAGNE

Pale straw appearance; soft, appealing, fruity nose; softening fruit on palate with mid-length, reflecting its minimum 10 years of age. **Fair to good.**

XO GRANDE CHAMPAGNE

Mid-straw hue; elegant, appealing, fruity, slightly sweet nose, showing fair wood tones; lively style on palate – supple with honey and hazel nut with long length; balanced; at least 20 years old. **Very good.**

TRÈS RARE

Mid-straw; softening, stylish, fruity nose with some elegance; softening palate with mid-length but a final harsh edge; minimum 50 years old. **Good.**

DUBOIGALANT TRÈS RARE GRANDE CHAMPAGNE
(WITH WAX TOP AND WIRE MESH ACROSS BOTTLE)

Pale orange core with long lemon rim; lightish nose with raisons, candied peel and subdued fruit; softening, fair fruit on palate, long length, real style with no harsh tones. **Very good.**

- RANGE -

ELÉGANCE GRANDE CHAMPAGNE

VSOP GRANDE CHAMPAGNE

XO GRANDE CHAMPAGNE

TRÈS RARE GRANDE CHAMPAGNE

DUBOIGALANT XO
GRANDE CHAMPAGNE

A. E. DUPUY

B.P. 62, 16102 Cognac
TEL: (33-5) 45 32 07 45
Visitors by appointment

Dupuy was founded in 1852 by Auguste Dupuy, who was succeeded by Edmond Dupuy in 1895. From the beginning, the company concentrated on the export market. Two Norwegians, Peter Rustad and Thomas Bache-Gabrielsen, bought the house in 1905, continuing with the Dupuy brand as well as selling cognac under the Bache-Gabrielsen label to Scandinavian countries. A direct descendant is still in charge: Christian Bache-Gabrielsen is managing director, assisted by Jean-Philippe Bergier.

Young cognac, amounting to 21,200 gallons, is purchased from four districts: 30 percent Grande Champagne, 20 percent Petite Champagne, 40 percent Fins Bois and 10 percent Bons Bois. This is derived 95 percent from Ugni Blanc with just 5 percent from the Colombard grape variety.

Dupuy has no stills. Limousin oak is used entirely with the raw spirit going into new casks and then being transferred into ones over 10 years of age. The Taransand cooperage in Cognac supplies the casks.

Sales of Three Star and VS account for 212,000 bottles, with VSOP for 23,000, Napoléon and Napoléon

DUPUY HORS D'AGE GRANDE
FINE CHAMPAGNE

Fine Champagne, 22,000, XO Fine Champagne for 30,000, and its two top cognacs–Extra Fine Champagne and Hors d'Age Grande Champagne for 10,000 bottles combined. The Extra Fine uses cognacs around 25 years old while the Hors d'Age has brandy of about 40 years old. The major markets are Japan, Norway (where Bache-Gabrielsen is brand leader), Belgium, Germany, Canada, Australia, Taiwan, and Hong Kong.

- **RANGE** -

DUPUY THREE STAR/
VS FINE CHAMPAGNE

DUPUY VSOP

DUPUY NAPOLÉON

DUPUY NAPOLÉON FINE
CHAMPAGNE

DUPUY XO FINE
CHAMPAGNE

DUPUY EXTRA FINE
CHAMPAGNE

DUPUY HORS D'AGE
GRANDE FINE
CHAMPAGNE

BACHE-GABRIELSEN
THREE STAR

BACHE-GABRIELSEN XO
FINE CHAMPAGNE

BACHE-GABRIELSEN
THOMAS XO FINE
CHAMPAGNE

ROCHAS NAPOLÉON

ROCHAS XO FINE
CHAMPAGNE

DUPUY EXTRA FINE CHAMPAGNE

The International Wine and Spirit Competition in the U.K. awarded the silver medal to Dupuy's Napoléon Fine Champagne. The Hors d'Age secured the gold award at the Segonzac competition.

The perfume House of Rochas has licensed Dupuy to make its cognac.

DUPUY SELECTION
FINE CHAMPAGNE

Tasting Notes

DUPUY SELECTION FINE CHAMPAGNE

Pale amber center and long ocher rim; not too clean nose — spirity, slightly nutty fruit; dry, light fruit on palate with rather fiery finish.
Fair.

DUPUY EXTRA FINE CHAMPAGNE

(PRESENTED IN AN ATTRACTIVE CYLINDRICAL CLEAR BOTTLE WITH TOP WIRED DOWN WITH SEAL)

Bright mid-tawny core with light pale ocher rim; nose shows warming fruit, some wood smoke, and licorice; lightish fruit, supple taste, balanced but slightly harsh final finish.
Good to very good.

DUPUY HORS D'AGE GRANDE FINE CHAMPAGNE

Mid- to deep-tawny appearance; smooth, fruity, and figs on nose, a little spirity; sweetish, honey palate with smooth figs, good length.
Very good.

EXSHAW

127 Boulevard Denfert Rochereau, 16100 Cognac
tel: (33-5) 45 36 88 88
No visitors

*J*ohn Exshaw founded the house which bears his name in 1805. He came from a noted Irish family and was a direct descendant of John Exshaw, Lord Mayor of Dublin in 1770.

Exshaw settled in Bordeaux in 1802 where his uncles were bankers. Three years later, he established a trade exporting wine and brandy from the Charente region. At that time, the English—as the major buyers of cognac—aged the spirit themselves. Exshaw considered the humid climate of the Atlantic coast of southwest France better suited for brandy

TRES RÀRE XO GRANDE CHAMPAGNE

maturation than England. To overcome the Continental blockade of Napoleon, he flew the American flag on his own vessels when exporting the spirit.

Exshaw was the first to ship cognac bottles to the Far East via Suez before the canal was even dug; the latter did not take place until 1859–69. Camels were used to transport the consignments across the Isthmus of Suez to Port Said!

Thomas-Henri, Exshaw's elder son, took over the trade, concentrating entirely on cognac. He personally selected the immature stock and supervised both its aging and blending. Exshaw became a leading brand on the world market with strong links in India, Burma, Malaysia, China, and West Africa. British decolonization and World War II eroded most of these contacts, and the firm was purchased by Otard in 1975.

Only wine from the Grande Champagne district, mainly Ugni Blanc, is used. Exshaw owns neither vineyards nor stills, but subcontracts to ten distilleries. The spirit is matured at 55–65 percent alcohol and aged 70 percent in Limousin oak and the balance in Allier oak; only 5 percent new wood is used. The casks are purchased from three different cooperages.

Sales in bottle are 57,000 for VSOP, 4,000 for XO No. 1 and 1,500 for Extra Age d'Or. The latter two are old cognacs aimed at the

Tasting Notes

TRÈS RARE XO GRANDE CHAMPAGNE

Mid-tawny hue; most appealing almonds and honey on the nose, some fruit, elegant; smooth, good fruit on palate with nutty edge, good length reflecting its 15–20 years age.
Very good.

EXTRA AGE D'OR TRÈS VIEILLE GRANDE CHAMPAGNE

Pale tawny core with wide pale ocher rim; light nose displaying apricots, honey, and nuts; fair fruit, quite rich palate, slightly nutty but harsh finish; twenty-five years old.
Fair to good.

connoisseur market and sell in leading restaurants, particularly in Belgium, the Netherlands, Germany, and France. Exshaw says it is the subtlety and lightness of the aromas on the latter two cognacs which really appeal to the cognac specialist. No competitions have recently been entered.

- RANGE -

TRÈS RARE XO
GRANDE
CHAMPAGNE

EXTRA AGE D'OR
TRÈS VIEILLE
GRANDE
CHAMPAGNE

AGE D'OR TRES VIEILLE
GRANDE CHAMPAGNE

Jean Luc FERRAND

ROUTE DU BOC, 16130 SEGONZAC
TEL: (33-5) 45 83 43 16
Visitors from 8.00AM–7.00PM

This family firm of grower-distillers was founded in the sixteenth century. Today it owns 64 acres at Segonzac, the heart of the Grande Champagne district, and proudly therefore states on the label "1er Cru de Cognac."

- **RANGE** -

VSOP

RÉSERVE

XO

Each year about 79,500 gallons wine are made using no grapes or wine other than from their own land, which is planted with Ugni Blanc. Two pot stills are used of 477 and 663 gallons, respectively. The spirit is aged in Allier and Limousin oak. France is its largest market. In addition to Pineau des Charentes (five-year-old white and rosé and a 10-year-old), Jean Luc Ferrand offers three qualities of cognac.

RÉSERVE GRANDE CHAMPAGNE

PINEAU
DES
CHARENTES

Appellation Pineau des Charentes Contrôlée

JEAN-LUC FERRAND
SARL JEAN-LUC FERRAND & FILS · 16130 SEGONZAC

SERVIR FRAIS

75 cl   PRODUCE OF FRANCE   17%vol.

VIEUX
PINEAU
DES
CHARENTES

Appellation Pineau des Charentes Contrôlée

JEAN-LUC FERRAND
SARL JEAN-LUC FERRAND & FILS · 16130 SEGONZAC

SERVIR FRAIS

75 cl   PRODUCE OF FRANCE ·   17%vol.

COGNAC
Grande Champagne
V.S.O.P.

1er Cru de Cognac
Appellation Grande Champagne Contrôlée

70 cl   JEAN-LUC FERRAND   40%vol.
SARL JEAN-LUC FERRAND & FILS · 16130 SEGONZAC
PRODUCE OF FRANCE

COGNAC
Grande Champagne
X.O.

1er Cru de Cognac
Appellation Grande Champagne Contrôlée

70 cl   JEAN-LUC FERRAND   40%vol.
SARL JEAN-LUC FERRAND & FILS · 16130 SEGONZAC
PRODUCE OF FRANCE

Tasting Note

RÉSERVE (40 PERCENT/VOL)

*Pale tawny core with long water ocher rim; nose
shows soft, stylish fruit; soft, supple palate with
good length, displaying fruit and hazel nuts.*
Very good.

Pierre FERRAND

LES CHARDONS LA NEROLLE, 16130 SEGONZAC
TEL: (33-5) 45 83 34 73
Visitors Monday—Friday 9.00AM—12 noon and 2.00—5.00PM

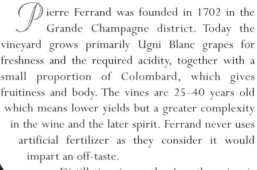

*P*ierre Ferrand was founded in 1702 in the Grande Champagne district. Today the vineyard grows primarily Ugni Blanc grapes for freshness and the required acidity, together with a small proportion of Colombard, which gives fruitiness and body. The vines are 25–40 years old which means lower yields but a greater complexity in the wine and the later spirit. Ferrand never uses artificial fertilizer as they consider it would impart an off-taste.

Distillation is on the *lees*; the wine is unfiltered, which imparts more aromas. Small pot stills are used with low necks to preserve the wine's aromas, resulting in a rounder, more fragrant cognac. Ferrand distills at a lower alcoholic strength–to 68 percent–instead of the more usual 71 percent, again to retain more of the aromas. Distillation is completed by December 31.

Small casks of 58–93 gallons of Limousin oak are used for its wider grain, rather than the tighter grained Tronçais. New wood for the young cognac is used for up to one year. *Redoullage* (restaving) is a technique developed at Ferrand. It uses old casks and replace a few staves with new oak every four years or so in order to have a very fine control over the tannin level in the cognac. In this way the cognac can breathe without becoming over-oaked or bitter.

PIERRE FERRAND'S HAND-BLOWN BOTTLE OF ABEL

Pierre Ferrand never blends maturing casks. When the cognac is nearly ready, it starts a slow reduction in the alcoholic strength. It takes 30-year-old cognac casks and fills them half-full with distilled water. Over time, the water absorbs some of the old cognac which has soaked into the wood. After about six months, the water has apparently attained 20 percent alcohol. This is then used to reduce the cognac— adding a little every three to six months and reducing by only 3 percent alcohol each time. The process takes up to six years, which could take just a few minutes with other producers.

Before bottling, each bottle is rinsed with a small amount of the same cognac which is then discarded. This prevents any bad odors combining with the carefully crafted spirit.

Pierre Ferrand's awards include the gold medal at the Challenge International du Vin in Blaye-Bourg (for Abel) and the CIVART Trophy.

Fine and Pale is an average six years, Ambre 10 years, Réserve 20 years. Sélection des Anges 30 years, Abel 45 years, and

PIERRE FERRAND SÉLÉCTION DES ANGES

Ancestrale 70 years. Ancestrale is limited to 300 bottles released each year. Abel is placed in hand-blown glass. Brut de Fut is not blended or reduced but reaches its 45–55 percent alcohol naturally with age; it is at least 25 years, with each bottle numbered and carrying the cask number.

Tasting Notes

AMBRE

Light ocher hue; very light, delicate floral nose; softening, light style, slightly bland, final bitter taste. **Fair.**

RÉSERVE

Pale straw appearance; round, delicate, mellow fruit on nose; fruity, some vanilla, stylish palate with walnuts, good length. **Good to very good.**

ABEL

Distinct tawny core with firm ocher rim; meaty, full, rich, many layered rancio nose; good spirity rich fruit on palate, much extract, long length and real depth. **Exceptional.**

ANCESTRALE

Light mahogany appearance; fair fruit, prunes, quite rich nose; rich, great extract on palate with underlying fruit, rather fiery edge, mid-length. **Good.**

PIERRE FERRAND ANCESTRALE

Jean FILLIOUX

LE POUYADE, 16130 JUILLAC-LE-COQ
TEL: (33-5) 45 83 04 09
Visitors by appointment

*F*ounded in 1880 by Honoré Fillioux, the company is now run by the great grandson, Pascal Fillioux. The vineyards are entirely in Grande Champagne and cover 54 acres, all planted in Ugni Blanc, because Pascal considers there is too much difficulty with *botrytis* in Folle Blanche.

The wines are distilled on the light *lees*; a *chauffe-vin* (heat exchanger) preheats the wine for 15 minutes before it is distilled. No *boisé* is used. Immediately after distillation, the alcoholic strength is reduced from 70 to 65 percent by volume. Only Limousin oak is selected "because it gives better tannins." New barrels of a maximum 93-gallon size are used for the first four to eight months; Pascal Fillioux likes the barrels to be only lightly charred to achieve maximum aromas.

Its awards include the gold medal from the 1979 International Wine & Spirit Competition for their Cep d'Or.

- **RANGE** -

COQ

LA POUYADE

NAPOLÉON

CEP D'OR

TRÈS VIEUX

RÈSERVE FAMILIALE

TRÈS
VIEUX

THE CHÂTEAU, IN THE HEART OF THE GRANDE CHAMPAGNE.

TASTING COGNAC AT FILLIOUX.

Tasting Notes

TRÈS VIEUX

Shows a pale tawny hue; good, inviting, stylish nose with evident wood; supple fruit, hint of almonds and style on the palate. **Overall, good.**

RÉSERVE FAMILIALE
(ALSO LABELED AS TRÈS VIEILLE)

Mid-ocher (with no caramel); a concentrated almond and vanilla nose, typical of rancio; the palate is soft with lovely fruit, stylish with good length. **Exceptional.**

JEAN FILLIOUX CEP D'OR GRANDE CHAMPAGNE

Mid-tawny core; plums on nose, slightly sweet; smooth, sweet palate, prunes, rather fiery edge. **Good.**

Alain FOUGERAT

LE BREUIL DE VOUHARTE, 16330 ST. AMANT DE BOIXE
TEL: (33-5) 45 39 01 16
Visitors by appointment

The Fougerat family has been vine-growers for five generations. Albert Fougerat planted vines on wasteland after his return from World War I. He constructed a warehouse and tile-lined cement vats to keep wine, and built a still in 1935.

Pierre Fougerat extended the vineyards, installed a new press in 1956, and a new still in 1965. At that time, most of their cognac was sold when it was two to three years old.

Today the vineyards at St. Amant de Boixe, northwest of Angoulême, lying partly on clay and partly on sand, are planted only with Ugni Blanc grapes. The harvest is still hand-picked. About 10,600 gallons wine is produced and distilled in a 398-gallon wood-heated boiler. The spirit—all from the Fins Bois district—is not reduced in alcoholic strength until two years before bottling. Under 0.8 percent sugar is added.

Maturation is entirely in Tronçais (Allier) oak casks, each of 80 to 106 gallons capacity with blending vats capable of taking 1,325 gallons. A little new wood is used for cognac intended for early sales, but Fougerat prefers casks of 8–15 years age in order that more vanilla and other finer characteristics naturally enrich the maturing spirit. The casks are purchased from Seguin Moreau in Merpins and from Chalufour in Jarnac.

THREE STAR

Tasting Notes

THREE STAR

Light, pale ocher hue, vanilla and hazelnuts, rather woody nose; hazelnut tones on palate, fruity and pungent. **Fair.**

XO

(PRESENTED IN APPEALING SQUARE-SHAPED DECANTER)

Bright, mid-tawny appearance; meaty, sweetish nose, a shade spirity; fruity, supple palate, some sweetness, tobacco, good length. **Good.**

In a typical year, sales in bottle are 2,720 Three Star, 1,450 VSOP, 540 Napoléon, 210 VR XO, and 100 Fine Cognac; the latter is at 50 percent alcohol, intended for eastern Europe and northern clients. The Fine is matured for 8 years, VSOP for 10 years, the Napoléon for 20 years, and the XO for 25 years. Sales are both local—to individuals and restaurants—and to the Netherlands, Germany, and Austria.

- **RANGE** -

THREE STAR

FINE

VSOP

NAPOLÉON

XO

ALAIN FOUGERAT XO

P. FRAPIN

B.P. 1, RUE PIERRE FRAPIN, 16130 SEGONZAC
TEL: (33-5)45 83 40 03
Visitors by appointment

*T*he Frapin family has been making wine and distilling cognac for over 20 generations. It can trace its Charentais base to 1270. Among its ancestors was the sixteenth-century writer François Rabelais, son of Antoine Rabelais and Catherine Frapin. This Benedictine monk and professor of anatomy is commemorated in Frapin's "Cuvée Rabelais" cognac.

In the 1690s, Pierre Frapin served as Royal apothecary to Louis XIV and was granted the family's coat-of-arms. His successor, Geneviève, is today president of the firm; Max Cointreau—for 35 years the guiding light at the liqueur-makers, Cointreau—is chairman, an appropriate rôle since he oversaw his first distillation in 1942 and today regularly tastes with Frapin's cellar master, Olivier Paultes; Béatrice Cointreau, educated at Paris and Cornell, is the energetic managing director as well as looking after Gosset champagne.

CHÂTEAU FONTPINOT GRANDE CHAMPAGNE TRÈS
VIEILLE RÉSERVE DU CHÂTEAU

Under Béatrice Cointreau's guiding hand, inventory management has been computerized, wine presses made pneumatic, and quality controlled through chromatographic analysis. Yet the traditions of cognac and Frapin in particular have been maintained, ensuring natural fermentation, traditional distillation on the *lees*, and long maturation periods.

Frapin owns the largest single estate in the Grande Champagne district, amounting to 741 acres of which 494 acres are under vine, while the average individually owned vineyard covers only 29.6 acres. The finest stock is on the 358 acres immediately adjacent to Château de Fontpinot. In the nearby town of Segonzac, the center of the Grande Champagne, are Frapin's offices.

On the friable limestone soil, which facilitates moisture-retention during the hot summer and aroma development, only cow manure is used on the young vines, spread 20 tons/acre. Frapin prefers training vines by the Double Guyot method (i.e. two canes and two spurs) rather than by Cordon (where there are alternating spurs to either side), since there are too many leaves with the latter and a danger of rot, even though it involves less manpower.

About 662,500 gallons wine is made from Ugni Blanc grapes. Folle Blanche is also planted, accounting for about 5 percent of the vineyard, but not currently used. Max Cointreau says that Folle Blanche was needed before *phylloxera* for its aromatic qualities but is being phased out since it can rot eight out of 10 years.

Frapin picks in early October, about a week earlier than other growers, to ensure more acidity, trying to obtain ¼ fl. oz per pint total acidity naturally. After a quick two hours of pressing, any leaves and pips are removed

VSOP GRANDE CHAMPAGNE

THE FRAPIN ESTATE IN GRANDE CHAMPAGNE.

by a sieve to ensure there is no excess astringency. Pneumatic presses are used for speed and no cultured yeasts employed. The wine is left unfiltered so that the aroma will retain its distinctive fruit.

The wine is then distilled with the *lees* (sediment) in one of Frapin's four copper stills, each holding 663 gallons. They use a *chauffe-vin* to ensure that there is no danger of cold wine entering the hot still. After the double distillation, the spirit is held at full strength for at least one year and then reduced by 8 degrees each two years, using a mix of cognac and distilled water. If cognac is reduced more quickly, it can smell soapy, maintains Max Cointreau.

The cognac is matured in Limousin oak because it releases both tannin and imparts "exotic" aromas (like coconut); the Cointreaus consider Allier/Tronçais wood neutral and therefore do not use it. Between one-third and one-quarter new casks are filled. A local cooper is employed. Unlike some houses, Frapin likes a light "toastiness" to the inside of their barrels.

- **RANGE** -

VS/THREE STAR

VSOP GRANDE CHAMPAGNE

NAPOLÉON GRANDE CHAMPAGNE

V.I.P. XO GRANDE CHAMPAGNE

DOMAINE FRAPIN VIEILLE GRANDE CHAMPAGNE

CHÂTEAU FONTPINOT GRANDE CHAMPAGNE TRÈS VIEILLE RÉSERVE DU CHÂTEAU

EXTRA RÉSERVE PATRIMONIALE PIERRE FRAPIN GRANDE CHAMPAGNE

CUVÉE RABELAIS

When sufficient tannins have been released, the cognac is transferred to older casks. During the maturation process, casks are moved from earth floors (where the air is damp) to warehouse attics (where the air is dry) and back again, according to their development. Frapin is justifiably proud of its substantial stocks, which ensure a high standard to the final range. Béatrice Cointreau stresses that Frapin has a very long cycle and should be thought of in "generations" (laying down stocks now for grandchildren and great-grandchildren yet unborn), rather than seen in annual agricultural cycles.

An associate firm (Château Paulet) bottles Frapin, much of which is packaged exquisitely. The V.I.P. XO is presented in an elegant sixteenth-century-style glass decanter, luxuriously mounted on a 24-carat gold base with matching stopper, while Frapin Extra comes in a fine crystal decanter. The Cuvée Rabelais is presented in a Baccarat crystal decanter, decorated with Renaissance emblems (peacock, book of knowledge, horn of plenty) engraved in 24-carat gold.

Fifty countries stock Frapin: 55 percent in Europe, 35 percent Asia and 10 percent America. The major markets are Germany, Belgium, Finland, France, Iceland, Sweden, Korea, Japan, the Philippines, Taiwan, and the U.S.A. Among the international awards achieved are from The International Wine and Spirit Competition (bronze medal for Domaine Frapin in 1993 and silver medal for the V.I.P. XO in 1996) and from the Chicago-based Beverage Testing Institute (platinum medal for Extra and silver medal for Château Fontpinot, both in 1996).

The only cognac sold by Frapin that is not exclusively Grande Champagne in origin is its VS/Three Star (standing for "Very Special"). This is based on Fins Bois and sold mainly in Scandinavia.

EXTRA RÉSERVE PATRIMONIALE PIERRE
FRAPIN GRANDE CHAMPAGNE

Tasting Notes

VSOP GRANDE CHAMPAGNE

Smooth, clean nose, honeyed with a hint of smoke; fair fruit on the palate, slightly harsh finish. Balanced. **Fair** *for being 10 years old*

DOMAINE FRAPIN VIEILLE GRANDE CHAMPAGNE
(KEPT ONE YEAR IN NEW OAK)

Soft, stylish, good-quality nose, quite smoky; palate shows lovely style with mid-length, reflecting an average 18–20 years of age. **Good to very good.**

CHÂTEAU FONTPINOT GRANDE CHAMPAGNE TRÈS VIEILLE RÉSERVE DU CHÂTEAU (41 PERCENT/VOLUME)
(AGED 6 MONTHS IN NEW OAK AND MATURED ON AVERAGE OVER 18–20 YEARS)

Nose shows a harder, slightly richer edge than Domaine Frapin; many-layered palate, again harder style (than Domaine Frapin), spirity with long length. **Good.**

V.I.P. XO GRANDE CHAMPAGNE
(FROM A DAMP CELLAR, COMPOSED OF COGNACS AROUND 35 YEARS OLD)

Nose shows a soft, elegant, many-layered style; good fruit and real length on palate. Balanced. **Very good.**

EXTRA RÉSERVE PATRIMONIALE PIERRE FRAPIN GRANDE CHAMPAGNE

Nose is heavier and softer than the V.I.P. XO; rich, rancio many-layered palate with mid-length. An evening cognac while enjoying V.I.P. XO for lunch! **Exceptional.**

CUVÉE RABELAIS
(A BLEND OF UGNI BLANC AND FOLLE BLANCHE OF WHICH 500 ONLY ARE BOTTLED)

Nose shows softening, really rich lovely fruit; great elegance on palate, many layers and depth, showing an exquisite smoky richness; long length. **Exceptional.**

GABRIEL et ANDREU

CHÂTEAU DE BONBONNET, 16130 ARS
TEL: (33-1) 30 24 52 48
*Visitors from Monday–Friday 9.00AM–12 noon and 2.00–5.00PM
or by appointment*

rs lies south of Cognac in the Petite Champagne district. Gabriel et Andreu produces four single-district cognacs with the aim of expressing each district's particular characteristics. Most cognac houses blend between districts, but Gabriel and Andreu seek the top vine growers in each district and work with them, using no chemical weed killers and requiring lower yields. The majority of the crop comes from old vines.

The wine is left on the *lees* during distillation to secure the maximum flavor and complexity. Distillation is completed in December to ensure the wine is still fresh, thereby retaining some of the clean, fresh fruit and floral aromas. Only small pot stills are used and the spirit matured in

- **RANGE** -

FINS BOIS
BORDERIES
PETITE CHAMPAGNE
GRANDE CHAMPAGNE

FINS BOIS

old Limousin oak, which has a wide grain and allows softer, more delicate cognacs to be produced. No caramel is ever added.

To reduce the alcoholic strength, small amounts of distilled water are added every 4 to 6 months over a 3 year period. Every bottle is rinsed with cognac of the same age before filling–a small detail but it means that Gabriel et Andreu cognacs remain pure. Each bottle is individually numbered and the lot given on the label, together with the date of bottling.

PETITE CHAMPAGNE

Tasting Notes

BORDERIES

Mid-ocher core with long, pale lemon rim; woody, soft fruit, hazel nut and jasmin tones on nose; fair fruit, a little hollow on palate, mid-length, with a rather harsh final edge. Bottled February 20, 1996. **Fair to good.**

PETITE CHAMPAGNE

Forty-two percent alcohol. Mid-straw core and long, pale lemon rim; light, delicate fruit, floral, appealing nose; stylish, light fruity taste, apricots and hazel nuts, no harsh tones. Mid-length. Bottled February 20, 1996. **Very good.**

GRANDE CHAMPAGNE

Forty-three percent alcohol. Mid-ocher core with pale lemon rim; appealing, good fruity nose, smoky, vanilla, many layers; good warming fruit on taste, fairly rich, elegant, mid-length, slightly harsh edge. Bottled May 29, 1996. **Very good.**

GAUTIER

Le Moulin du Château, 28 rue des Ponts, B.P. 3,
16140 Aigre
tel: (33-5) 45 21 10 02
Visitors by appointment

*C*harles Gautier married the daughter of a wine producer in Aigre in 1644. Their grandson, Louis, secured a royal warrant to produce cognac in 1755. The charter, signed by Louis XV, is still at the headquarters today and ever since then the firm has been managed by direct descendants of the Gautier family.

Gautier purchases from Cognac's first four growths, excluding Bons Bois and Bois Communs. It has no still of its own, buying young spirit which it ages in both Limousin and Tronçais oak in its warehouses in the center of the town of Aigre, continually lapped on the cellar line by the slowly flowing water. This keeps the temperature constant while the humidity ensures only a subtle evaporation.

Ninety-four percent of Gautier's production is exported to over 65 countries, particularly Russia, the U.S., Canada, Taiwan, Japan, South Korea, Poland, Belgium, the Netherlands, and the U.K. Before World War I, it was not uncommon to see horse-drawn wagons bearing the coat-of-arms of its more illustrious clients trundling through the gates to reach cellars in Prague, Vienna, and St. Petersburg.

Gautier sells 1 million bottles annually: 50 percent VS/Three Star, 30

GAUTIER VSOP

Tasting Notes

VSOP VIEILLE

Mid-tawny hue; smooth, toasted almonds on nose; softening, fair fruit on palate. **Fair to good.**

XO GOLD

(PRESENTED IN A TRIANGULAR-SHAPED BOTTLE)

Mid-tawny core with long, pale lemon rim; very stylish, good woody fruit, displaying many tones on nose, some apricot and vanilla; smooth, good fruity palate, no harsh tones, good length. **Very good.**

TRADITION RARE

(NUMBERED BOTTLES)

Mid-tawny core; lovely toasted-almond nose with style; elegant fruity taste, good length, supple. **Very good.**

percent VSOP, and 20 percent in superior qualities, all at 40 percent alcohol. The range has won many awards: in 1989 the VSOP won the bronze medal at The International Wine and Spirit Competition in the U.K., in 1993 the Napoléon secured the bronze medal at the same event, in 1993 the XO obtained the silver award at Vinexpo, and in 1994 the XO Gold secured the bronze at The International Wine and Spirit Competition.

- RANGE -

VS/THREE STAR

VSOP

NAPOLÉON

XO GOLD

TRADITION RARE

GAUTIER XO GOLD

COGNAC
GAUTIER

TRADITION RARE

GAUTIER PRESENTATION BOX

Paul GIRAUD

16120 BOUTEVILLE
TEL: (33-5) 45 97 03 93
Visitors welcome daily 1.30–5.30PM. Guided tours by appointment

*T*he Giraud family have been vine-growers since 1650. Its vineyards cover 86.5 acres–74 acres owned and the balance rented–on the eastern side of the Grande Champagne district in the villages of Bouteville and St. Même les Carrières.

Growing Ugni Blanc almost entirely (5 percent Folle Blanche, which Paul Jean Giraud's father felt made a better spirit although it suffers more from rot), the vines are planted about 4 feet apart and in rows about 10 feet wide. A water-pressure drill is used to plant vines because the ground is so stony.

Unlike most of the region, Giraud still picks by hand; he estimates only two percent is still hand-picked in the Grande Champagne. This used to be undertaken by Spanish workers based near Bezièrs in southern France but now by local villagers. In fact, there are 50 vine-growers in Bouteville.

He is one of about 20 farmers in Cognac who use biological methods in the vineyard

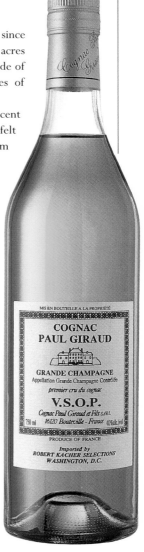

PAUL GIRAUD VSOP

with an absolute minimal amount of chemical sprays. An experimental 14.8-acre plot is being treated totally biologically, only using sulfur dioxide and two copper sulfate sprays. A label symbol indicating biological practice cannot be applied as the rest of the vineyards are not treated in that way. Giraud feels that it would be too risky if wet conditions (requiring chemical treatments) were encountered.

- RANGE -

VSOP

NAPOLÉON

VIEILLE RÉSERVE XO

TRÈS RARE

A pneumatic press is used with the stalks left intact. An 8–10 percent wine results using natural yeasts–high in acidity which keeps it in good condition throughout any cold weather until distillation. Usually Giraud waits until the malolactic fermentation is complete and then uses two pot stills with a capacity of 371 gallons, bought in 1950 and 477 gallons acquired in 1962. Two distillations are completed every 24 hours, requiring Giraud to have a temporary camp bed set up for the night. With gas heating (instead of a fire) and automatic controls, the first distillation need only be checked every seven hours, and every 30 minutes during the second distillation.

PAUL GIRAUD VIEILLE RÈSERVE XO

Tasting Notes

VSOP

Spirity fruit on nose; youthful, although eight years old; palate has a rather harsh spirity edge. **Fair.**

NAPOLÉON

Lovely, warming fruit, inviting nose, combining "flower and fruit"; warm, supple palate with good fruit; mid-length reflecting its average 15-year age. **Good to very good.**

VIEILLE RÉSERVE

Soft, delicate, sweetish nose — like stone fruit; palate shows subtle, honeyed fruit; mid- to long-length, showing its 25-year age. **Very good.**

TRÈS RARE

Very soft complex nose, slight cloves and pepper; warm, mid-length palate with slightly peppery final edge. A true reflection of a 35-year-old cognac. **Very good.**

A *chauffe-vin* to prewarm the wine is used but care is taken to ensure it does not exceed 30°C (86°F). Distillation is on the *lees*, which Giraud considers important for quality when making Grande Champagne and aiming for old cognac. Yet using the *lees* creates a further complication as too great a quantity can result in a cooked taste in the raw spirit.

The cognac is matured at full strength. Limousin oak is preferred to Tronçais with 30 percent new wood—using quality seasoned barrels—and long aging in their very humid warehouse. In his *chai*, cognac loses 20 percent alcohol over a decade. No *boisé* is introduced as Giraud wishes to make as pure a cognac as possible.

One quarter of production is sold on three-year contracts to two houses: for 10 years Giraud has supplied Hennessy and for 20 years Rémy-Martin. Under its own name, its major markets are Japan, Germany, the U.S., and the Netherlands.

Its awards include the gold medal at the 1981 Basle Concours International de Spiriteux for the Napoléon and the Distinction d'Honneur at the same competition for the Vieille Réserve.

GODET FRÈRES

1 RUE DU DUC, B.P. 41, 170003 LA ROCHELLE
TEL: (33-5) 46 41 10 66
Visitors Monday–Friday from 2.30–4.30PM

*I*n 1550, Bonaventure Godet, a Dutch merchant, settled in the port of La Rochelle and started trading in the salt and wines of the region. In 1730, Augustin Godet exported cognac to both the Dutch and English courts. The company was established in 1782 and is now managed by the eighth generation of the family.

Young cognac is purchased 50 percent from Grande Champagne, 20 percent each from Fins Bois and Borderies, with the balance coming from Bons Bois and Petite Champagne. Godet Frères let the spirit reduce in alcoholic strength naturally and age 30 percent in new wood. Only Tronçais oak is used. Stocks amount to a 10-years turnover.

One million bottles are sold annually of which 95 percent is exported to 45 countries with a keen

Tasting Notes

EXCELLENCE

Pale tawny appearance; delicate, fruity, vanilla nose; palate shows softening fruit – cherries – with a hint of truffles and a rather fiery finish. **Good.**

RÉSERVE DE LA FAMILLE EXTRA VIEILLE GRANDE CHAMPAGNE
(PRESENTED WITH A WAX-SEAL TOP AND WIRE MESH ACROSS THE BOTTLE)

Amber core with wide, pale lemon rim; smoky fruit on nose, buttery and rancio; softening, good fruit on palate with real style, long length, quite rich, balanced. **Very good.**

GODET FRÈRES EXCELLENCE

- RANGE -

CUVÉE JEAN GODET
THREE STAR

SÉLÉCTION SPÉCIALE

GASTRONOME

NAPOLÉON

EXCELLENCE

XO

RÉSERVE DE LA
FAMILLE EXTRA
VIEILLE GRANDE
CHAMPAGNE

demand in Taiwan. It does not sell through supermarkets.

Among the competitions won, Godet Frères secured the gold medal at the 1990 Brussels Monde Selection and silver award five years later at The International Wine & Spirit Competition held in the U.K. for its Excellence brand. Their XO also won the gold award at the 1994 Brussels Monde Selection.

The Cuvée Jean Godet Three Star is a blend of Fins Bois, Borderies, and Bons Bois, accounting for 15 percent of sales. The Séléction Spéciale is a blend of six- to eight-year-old Bons Bois and Fins Bois, described as being "mellow and slightly woody with a touch of hazel nut, stewed peaches, and red fruits." It is a superior VSOP and accounts for half their sales.

Gastronome was invented in 1920; it is a blend of eight Grande Champagnes and some Petite Champagne. It forms 5 percent of sales. The Napoléon is a blend of over 15-years-old Fins Bois, Borderies, and Bons Bois. Excellence is a blend of over 25-years-old Grande Champagne, Borderies, and Petite Champagne; it is positioned between Napoléon and XO, accounting for one-fifth of sales.

The XO is a blend of over 30-years-old Grande and Petite Champagnes, accounting for 5 percent of sales. The top of the range for Godet Frères is its Grande Champagne, which is over half a century old.

RÉSERVE DE LA FAMILLE EXTRA VIEILLE
GRANDE CHAMPAGNE

Léopold GOURMEL

La Couture, B.P. 16130 Gente, Cognac
tel: (33-5) 45 83 76 60
Visitors daily by appointment

*L*éopold Gourmel was founded in the late 1970s by Pierre Voisin and Olivier Blanc, following many years of hobby blending by Voisin. In 1990 the company was sold to a bank and purchased back in 1993 by Blanc.

With the exception of the old stock, Gourmel is made from one vineyard of 81.51 acres located at Hiersac in the Fins Bois. Only the Ugni Blanc is cultivated but experiments are taking place with both Colombard and Folle Blanche. The still lies at the vineyard and distillation takes place on the *lees*, using a *chauffe-vin* to preheat the wine.

> - **RANGE** -
>
> Age du Fruit
> Age des Fleurs
> Age des Épices
> Quintessence

AGE DES EPICES FINS BOIS

Great care is taken over the selection of oak. A Segonzac cooper makes the casks and some of their staves are sold to other coopers. Distillation is completed by the end of February and all the young spirit is placed in new wood for up to nine months. Only Tronçais oak is used, which is selected north-west of Bourges and east of Amboise.

The spirit is matured around 68 percent for five years. It is then gradually reduced using a mix of cognac and distilled water. No *Boisé*, caramel or syrup is added.

Although the vineyard is not owned by Gourmel, the company has an option to purchase it if it comes on the market. Traditions are respected, such as the continuance of picking grapes by hand. Blanc hopes to introduce single vintage cognacs. The company is based at Genté, due south of Cognac.

Tasting Notes

AGE DU FRUIT

Bright mid-straw appearance; flowery, elegant style on nose but slight spirity oilyness; supple fair fruit on palate with fair acidity; mid length, reflecting its eight years' age.
Fair to good.

AGE DES FLEURS

Bright, mid-straw core with pale ocher rim; nose initially dumb, but second nose shows slightly heavy, dull fruit with rancio hint; warm fruit on palate, reflecting average 12 years' age but spirity finish.
Fair to good.

AGE DES ÉPICES

Bright, mid-straw core with pale ocher rim; nose shows heavy fruit, dull, oily; quite rich palate of average 20 years with heavy dull fruit. Good length. **Good.**

QUINTESSENCE

Pale tawny core with wide pale ocher rim; nose shows heavy rancio style, indicative of over 30 years' maturity; supply fair fruit, some almonds on palate. **Fair to good.**

GOURSAT-GOURRY de Chadeville

DOMAINE DE CHADEVILLE, 67 RUE GASTON BRIAND,
16130 SEGONZAC
TEL: (33-5) 45 83 39 49
Visitors by appointment

*S*ince 1619, the Gourry family has owned Domaine de Chadeville, situated at Segonzac in the center of the Grande Champagne district. Using only its own vineyards, Goursat-Gorry makes about 21,200 gallons wine annually from the Ugni Blanc grape and distills on site, securing 2.2 pints of spirit for every 19.8 pints wine.

The cognac is supervised by Pierre Goursat-Gourry, using Limousin wood of 15–20 years of age for maturing the spirit. He likes to secure cinnamon and vanilla aromas. About 10,000 bottles are sold: 5,000 VSOP (eight years), 3,000 Très Vieux (25 years), and 2,000 XO (35 years). The production from the oldest family vine-grower in the area is sold in France, Germany, the U.S., and Asia.

- **RANGE** -

VSOP CHADEVILLE

TRÈS VIEUX

XO

XO GRANDE CHAMPAGNE

Tasting Notes

GOURSAT-GOURRY VSOP CHADEVILLE

Amber core; woody / vanilla nose with some fruit; woody fruit on palate, fair style, mid-length. **Good.**

GOURSAT-GOURRY XO

(PRESENTED WITH WAX SEAL)

Light mahogany core, tight mid-ocher rim; nose shows marzipan and odd wood; palate shows wood overpowering the fruit, mid-length. **Fair to good.**

GOURSAT-GOURRY TRÈS VIEUX

(WAX SEAL WITH DRIVEN CORK – NOT PRACTICAL FOR LATER USE)

Deep caramel core with tight ocher rim; spirity, fruity nose with some wood; unripe, slightly coarse fruit on palate, too spirity. **Fair.**

UGNI BLANC GRAPES.

VSOP GRANDE FINE CHAMPAGNE

GUERBÉ

16130 JUILLAC-LE-COQ
TEL: (33-5) 45 83 67 06
Visitors by appointment from Monday–Friday at 9.00AM–12 noon and 2.00–6.00PM

*G*uerbé is a family company, using only its own Ugni Blanc grapes. Originally, part of the vineyard's crop at Juillac-le-Coq in the Grande Champagne district was sold to the larger *négociants*. Daniel Guerbé, son of the founder (Jean), is president.

The vineyard covers 103.7 acres and is today managed by Daniel Guerbé's son, Jean, while his daughter, Marie Christine, has responsibility for commercial activities. Some 153,700 gallons wine are distilled on the estate at Logis de Puyguiller.

Only Limousin oak is used for aging; the spirit goes into new wood for the first six months and is then transferred into old barrels with an average age of 10 years. The casks are purchased from the Allary cooperage at Archiac.

VSOP GRANDE CHAMPAGNE

- **RANGE** -

VS

VSOP

RARE RÉSERVE

NAPOLÉON

XO

EXTRA

GRANDE RÉSERVE

VIEILLE

In bottle, Guerbé sell annually about 3,000 VS, 17,000 VSOP, 16,000 Rare Réserve, 1,700 Napoléon, 35,000 XO and Extra, 1,000 Grande Réserve, and 500 Vieille Grande Champagne. In addition, 5,000 bottles Pineau des Charentes are made, recommended by Guerbé as both an apéritif and to accompany certain dishes.

Most sales are in France but also in Germany, Sweden, Taiwan, Hong Kong, and Malta. Guerbé won fourth prize for an old Grande Champagne cognac at the 1993 Concours.

VS GRANDE FINE CHAMPAGNE

Tasting Notes

VS GRANDE CHAMPAGNE

Pale straw; elegant, lovely, fruity nose; warm, stylish fruit on palate, mid-length. **Very good.**

VSOP GRANDE CHAMPAGNE

Mid-tawny hue; light, fruity nose with prunes; softening fruity taste, a shade fiery, mid-length. **Good.**

RARE RÉSERVE GRANDE CHAMPAGNE
(BOTTLED IN ATTRACTIVE HEART-SHAPED DECANTER)

Mid-straw hue with long, pale brown rim; nose shows oily aromas of young spirit; softening fair fruit on palate with fiery final edge. **Fair to good.**

XO GRANDE CHAMPAGNE
(BOTTLED IN THE SAME DECANTER AS THE RARE RÉSERVE)

Pale tawny core with long, pale ocher rim; vanilla and softening fruit on nose with many layers; appealing soft, good fruity taste, many-layered. Real quality and good length. **Exceptional.**

XO GRANDE CHAMPAGNE

A. HARDY

142 RUE BASSE DE CROUIN, B.P. 27, 16100 COGNAC
TEL: (33-5) 45 82 59 55
No visitors

*A*nthony Hardy founded the company in 1863. A London importer, he moved to Cognac to have better control of his stocks. The family has continued the trade and is now run by the fifth generation. When British sales fell in the late nineteenth century following an excise duty rise, Hardy closed its London office and concentrated instead on central Europe (Vienna, Prague, Berlin), Oslo, and Russia. For a time, Hardy supplied the Russian Czars using the special name, the "Cognac de l'Alliance."

Initially the family owned vineyards, but a later generation sold them to concentrate on purchasing wine, which it distills, and spirit. Francis Hardy, the current mayor of Cognac, trained his son, Patrick, to taste and select.

Around 1.5 million bottles are produced annually. As a small family house, Hardy blends according to its customers' taste. The VS is blended from the Fins Bois (where the early maturing qualities lend it round-ness) and the Borderies (which enhances the structure and aromas); the label design is based on the firm's own visiting card which, by tradition, has a corner turned down when the caller is a personal friend. Hardy considers its VSOP Fine Champagne the "greatest test of quality"; it has 10 years aging and carries the house symbol–the rooster.

Hardy considers its XO its flagship cognac. It is blended from the two inner districts of Grande and Petite Champagne,

VSOP FINE CHAMPAGNE

using 25-year-old cognacs. "Noces d'Or" was first blended in 1946; it uses only Grande Champagne with an average age of half a century to impart harmony and balance. It is packed in a box made from wild-cherry wood. The Noces de Diamond (Diamond) also de-rives exclusively from the Grande Cham-pagne district, using very old cognacs. It is aged for a minimum 60 years. The Noces de Perle (Pearl) is at least 30 years old and again comes from the Grande Champagne. Both "Pearl" and "Diamond" are packed in Kaspar crystal de-canters. Hardy's highest quality, Perfection, includes some cognac distilled before *phylloxera* devastated the region's vines (pre-1870); it is released every 10 to 20 years and bottled at 41 percent alcohol. The house also produces a white, rosé, and 10-year-old Pineau des Charentes.

- RANGE -

VS

VSOP FINE CHAMPAGNE

NAPOLÉON

XO

NOCES D'OR

PERFECTION

Tasting Notes

A. HARDY VSOP FINE CHAMPAGNE

Deep gold core with wide mid ocher rim; inviting woody fruit on nose with some rancio character; light fruity taste, no harsh tones, short length. **Good.**

A. HARDY "RED CORNER" THREE STAR

Pale tawny core, long pale ocher rim; young sappy wood, not appealing nose, not fiery; fair fruit on palate, vanilla, fair acidity, mid length. **Fair to good.**

VS "RED CORNER"

JAS. HENNESSY

1 RUE DE LA RICHONNE, 16101 COGNAC
TEL: (33-5) 45 35 72 72

*Visitors (with guided tours in several languages) from January–May and
October–December on Monday–Friday at 8.30–11.00AM and 1.45–4.30PM;
June–September on Monday–Saturday at 9.30AM–5.30PM
(excluding public holidays)*

*H*ennessy was founded in 1765 by an Irishman, Richard Hennessy, a captain in the Irish Brigade of the King of France, Louis XV. His first consignment of cognac was to Ireland and Britain, and, in the following year, 13,000 dozen bottles were shipped to French colonies in America.

Richard Hennessy's son, Jacques, succeeded as head of the firm, giving it the name "Jas. Hennessy." Since then, six successive generations of the family have become president. Today, a direct descendant of the founder, Henri de Pracomtal, presides. In 1971, the firm merged with the champagne house, Moët et Chandon, and with Christian Dior perfumes. Together with Louis Vuitton, Hennessy now forms part of the luxury goods company, LVMH, which also owns Hine Cognac.

Hennessy has always enjoyed an important export trade. In 1794, it made its first shipment to New York, followed four years later by the first stocks to Germany. In 1817, the prince regent (the future King George IV) ordered an "excellent old pale *eau-de-vie* of Cognac" from Hennessy; this

HENNESSY PRIVILEGE VSOP

became VSOP. Later Maurice Hennessy was the first to bottle cognac in the town. He also invented a grading system in 1865, using stars to designate different quality levels – a system soon adopted by the rest of the trade.

The XO top quality was devised in 1870 and the first shipments made two years later to China and Ireland. The distinctive decanter shape was introduced in 1947. In recent times Hennessy has created several cognacs: Paradis (1979) and four in 1995–Choice (for China), Bras d'Or and Extra (duty-free), and Privé (designed for consumption in the Japanese home); in 1996, Richard Hennessy, in honor of the founder, was launched.

Hennessy has taken a leading rôle in developing the promotional and quality control aspects of cognac, creating the Bureau de Répartition du Cognac during the German occupation of Cognac in World War II. This evolved into today's Bureau National Interprofessionnel du Cognac (BNIC).

The company and other members of the Hennessy family own 1,556 acres of vineyards but, once distilled, the spirit accounts for just over 2 percent of their needs. Although the grape yield can be high, such as 1,390 gallons per acre, in 1996, the amount authorized to be made into cognac may be far less (748 gallons/acre in 1996).

To supplement Hennessy's requirements, some 2,600 vine-growers are contracted and controlled by the firm's research and quality-

HENRI DE PRACOMTAL, PRESIDENT OF HENNESSY.

A ST. LOUIS CRYSTAL DECANTER OF RICHARD HENNESSY,
AN EXCEPTIONAL COGNAC.

control laboratory, founded in the 1950s. The aim is to secure very clean-flavored wines, almost entirely from the Ugni Blanc vine, which is fermented at 68–76.6°F for five to six days. As the Ugni Blanc ripens late, it needs to be picked quickly, and so mechanical harvesting is now the norm. A fast pressing, taking only around two hours, follows with the stalks intact.

Distillation is at 27 sites of which Hennessy owns three: two are on the outskirts of Cognac and the third at Juillac le Coq in the heart of the Grande Champagne district. The firm distills off the *lees* but uses a *chauffe-vin* to save fuel (40 percent of its gas costs have been saved); this process heats the wine for the last two hours of the distillation. some 50 percent of Hennessy's purchases by volume are as immature spirit, excluding the two outlying districts of Bons Bois and Bois Communs.

Only Limousin oak selected from forests in central France form the barrels for maturing Hennessy cognac. The trees selected are a minimum century-old and, to ensure continuity of supply, the firm has purchased 1,112 acres whose trees will mature by the year 2020.

In 1972, the Taransaud cooperage, which dates from 1672, was purchased by Hennessy. Its coopers mature the broad-grained Limousin oak for three years before selecting 32 staves to make each barrel. This aging allows the vanilla flavor to develop. Together with the Garnier cooperage, which is also owned by Hennessy, each barrel is given 12–14 minutes heating over a fire to obtain a medium to heavy "toasty" quality. The capacity is usually 93 gallons but larger at

- RANGE -

VS

PRIVILÈGE VSOP

CHOICE

PRIVÉ

BRAS D'OR

XO

EXTRA

PARADIS

RICHARD HENNESSY

146 gallons if the barrel is required to age old cognacs of at least 50 years. The cooperages not only supply Hennessy's needs but also supply leading estates in Bordeaux, Australia, California, New Zealand, and South Africa.

The raw spirit is placed initially in new wood and stored in one of 42 warehouses which collectively carry over 250,000 barrels.

Hennessy claims to be the only cognac firm to carry out both a qualitative as well as a quantitative check on its stock. For five months, the cellar master, Yann Fillioux, and his team taste the entire stock and decide on a barrel's next location (into, for example, a drier or more humid warehouse) and the evolutionary stage with the eventual blending in mind, according to the "cru" (district), origin, and age.

There is no humidity control and the spirits are stored at full distillation strength. They are reduced with distilled water at the blending stage. The oldest stock dates from 1800 (now in a glass demijohn) while the oldest cognac still in barrel originates from the 1872 vintage. Blending is made late in the cycle. *Boisé* is not introduced specifically at Hennessy, but it cannot tell if it has been applied to spirits purchased in.

Hennessy exports over 2.62 million cases, equivalent to 31.5 million bottles, to 120 countries. With a turnover in 1995 of 5.3 billion French francs, it is the leading cognac company, shipping 28.5 percent of the total market. Its major sales are in the U.S., Japan, China, duty-free, Ireland, Malaysia, Singapore, the U.K., and Germany. The company is joint owner of Cognac Davidoff which produces a VSOP and an Extra. It has

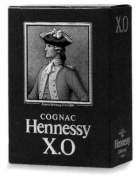

BOX OF HENNESSY XO

two affilitated cognac firms: Thomas Hine of Jarnac and Monnet, which formerly belonged to the family of Jean Monnet, "the father of Europe." Hennessy does not sell either in bulk or under its own label.

Visitors have been welcomed for many years, and in 1996 an instructive and original visitor center, called Les Quais Hennessy, was built. Designed by Jean-Michel Wilmotte, the museum explores the traditions of making cognac in a modern setting. Visitors usually start the informative tour by first crossing the Charente river by boat to see the warehouses on the opposite bank.

One of the distinguishing features of Hennessy is its use of the family coat-of-arms: an arm and broadax.

HENNESSY XO

Tasting Notes

VS

Bright, mid-tawny core with wide ocher rim; initially fruity nose showing soome wood, light hazel nuts and spirity overtones; spirity warming fruit on palate, evident oak but a harsh final edge. **Fair.**

PRIVILÈGE VSOP

Similar appearance as VS; softening fruit with wood and slightly clumsy vanilla on nose; taste shows softening spirit, woody fruit, mid-length, with a spirity final edge. **Fair to good.**

BRAS D'OR

Similar appearance to VS; quite soft nose with fair fruit and smoky hint; some fruit but harsh edge on palate and short length. **Fair.**

XO
(PRESENTED IN AN ATTRACTIVE SQUAT BOTTLE, EMBOSSED WITH GRAPE BUNCHES)

Quite deep tawny core with tight distinct ocher rim; fair fruit on nose with soft appealing wood tones, smoky, stylish; palate shows softening fruit, again good wood influence, mid-length, but slightly harsh final taste. Balanced. **Good.**

EXTRA
(LABELED "EXTRA RARE" NOSTALGIE DE BAGNOLET, PRESENTED IN A SQUAT BOTTLE WITH EMBOSSED GRAPE BUNCHES)

Appearance similar to XO; nose shows soft, fair fruit with rich second tones; softening, good fruit and extract on palate, appealing soft edge, mid-length. **Very good.**

PARADIS "RARE COGNAC"
(PRESENTED IN AN APPEALING DECANTER)

Tawny core with distinct ocher rim; soft, stylish light fruit on nose with no harsh tones, good hint of mature wood; quite rich palate, mellowing and evident wood, mid-length. This cognac is based on the very old reserves. **Very good.**

RICHARD HENNESSY
(PRESENTED IN A St. LOUIS CRYSTAL DECANTER WITH SAND-BLASTED EDGING DEPICTING VINE LEAVES AND GRAPE BUNCHES)

Mid-tawny appearance with long distance ocher rim; inviting fruity nose, soft, subtle and appealing; soft, stylish palate, mellow with no harsh tones, long length and lovely balance. A truly worthy cognac to honor Hennessy's founder. **Exceptional.**

Thomas HINE

16 Quai de l'Orangerie, 16200 Jarnac
tel: (33-5) 45 35 59 59
No visitors

Thomas Hine was born in Beaminster in Dorset, England, in 1775 and went on an exchange visit to France in 1793 to learn the French language. He was the guest of an old established Jarnac family, but when the Revolution was declared, Thomas was imprisoned in a wing of the Château de Jarnac, along with a ship's captain, John Pearson, who had been regularly shipping cognac. Released after a few months, Hine fell in love with a local girl, Françoise Elisabeth Delamain, whom he married.

Hine was made a partner in his father-in-law's business. He developed a reputation for seeking only the finest cognac and, in time, the company adopted his name. He sat on Jarnac town council and became its mayor, possibly the first Englishman to be elected to this post in any French town. Although he had arrived in the district as a youth, by the age of 47 he became the second largest taxpayer in the canton.

SIGNATURE PETITE CHAMPAGNE

Thomas Hine died in 1822. Today the sixth generation presides. The firm's logo, a deer, was created in 1866. In that year, Thomas Georges Hine wrote, "We need something other than our name on our cases. I suggest we adopt a deer."

Until the mid-nineteenth century, Hine shipped its cognac in 71 gallons made of oak from the Limousin forest. Gradually the firm switched to exporting in bottle (although it has retained its tradition of shipping small quantities in bulk for "early landed vintage cognac"). The 1850–1900 era saw the flat, horse-drawn barges, known as "gabares," carry wooden cases in place of casks.

In 1971, Hine became part of the Distillers Company and, in turn, Guinness. By corporate stages, this now forms part of the luxury LVMH group whose partners include Moët Champagne and Hennessy Cognac.

Hine owns no vineyards and no stills. It purchases spirit, about half when it is very young and the balance when reasonably mature. Most is obtained from the Grande and Petite Champagne districts with a small amount from the Fins Bois. Immediately after distillation, Hine likes to reduce the strength to 60 percent alcohol, because if left at the full 70 percent, the spirit penetrates too

TRIOMPHE GRANDE CHAMPAGNE

deeply into the wood and absorbs excessive amounts of tannin, according to Bernard Hine.

Only Trançais oak is used at Hine. "Use Limousin wood if you wish to sell young cognac," says Bernard Hine. Most of their barrels are 93 gallons but a few are 72 gallons capacity. The casks are entirely made by hand without glue or nails. Before use, they are scalded with hot water and seasoned with cognac.

The Hine warehouse lies alongside the river Charente in Jarnac. There is a minimum 80 percent relative humidity. New casks are used for the first eight months and then the cognac is matured in seasoned wood. No *boisé* is allowed. The development is therefore entirely natural. Hine ages its cognac in separate batches and places great emphasis on regular tasting to check on comparative development.

The art of blending reaches a high form at the house of Hine. Great care is taken to harness the individual aromatic qualities and to marry them to appropriate stylish tastes to ensure overall harmony and balance. Once a blend (or "assemblage") has been identified, the resulting cognac is retained in vat for a further 10–12 months so that the various components are unified. A final filtering is given prebottling with the bottles actually rinsed in cognac! Bottles are individually examined against a light after filling and a reference sample of every release retained for a decade.

The major markets are the U.K., U.S., Germany, Hong Kong, Taiwan, China, and duty-free. Hine supplies such French specialists as Fauchon, Nicolas, and the Savour Club. All sales in bottle are at 40 percent alcohol by volume.

Hine is the only cognac house to hold the British Royal warrant. It is the appointed cognac supplier to Queen Elizabeth II.

Early landed cognac is one of Hine's specialities. It is a tradition which dates back to

FAMILY RÈSERVE GRANDE CHAMPAGNE

- **RANGE** -

SIGNATURE PETITE
CHAMPAGNE

RARE & DELICATE
FINE CHAMPAGNE

NAPLOLÉON OLD
RÉSERVE

ANTIQUE TRÈS RARE
FINE CHAMPAGNE

XO

EXTRA

TRIOMPHE GRANDE
CHAMPAGNE

FAMILY RÉSERVE
GRANDE
CHAMPAGNE

the eighteenth century when British wine merchants would import one- to three-year-old cognac and age them in the damp vaulted cellars of Bristol or London under the control of Customs and Excise.

Today small quantities are still shipped in this way, occasionally to celebrate an event (such as a birth or marriage) but more often by a group of people, sometimes as part of a merchant's cellar scheme. Hine checks on the maturity and recommends the date for bottling, usually 15–25 years after shipment. Comparing Grande Champagne cognacs that have been matured in Cognac and the U.K. respectively, the former showed more fruit and depth while the latter was more delicate.

The choice of vintage can play a substantial part in the development of such an early landed cognac. If 1952 is taken—a cold, acidic year—the resulting cognac acquires a fine, delicate quality over the ensuring quarter-century. Yet a warm summer like 1953 results in a fruitier, richer cognac. Such factors need to be considered before purchasing particular years. As early landed is warehoused on a duty-free basis, HM Customs and Excise permit the "angels' share" of evaporation and only charge on the reduced volume that is actually bottled.

Until recently, cognac distillers and blenders were unable to legally label a bottle with a specific vintage. However, since 1988 it has been possible for warehouses to be double-locked, one lock each held by the distiller/blender and French excise offical respectively. The intention is that such stock will be held for at least 15 years.

Hine emphasizes that, unlike wine, cognac does not age in bottle but exclusively in cask. It warns against dusty bottles: "Experience shows that the quality of the cognac often suffers from a long storage in bottle, especially if lying on their side in contact with the cork." Hine advises that the average aging period for Signature is six years, for Rare & Delicate 10 years, for Antique 20–25 years, Triomphe 45 years, and for Family Réserve Grande Champagne 60–70 years. The Napoléon Old Réserve and XO are sold at duty-free stores. Both the vintages, and bottling dates of Hine early landed cognac will vary.

ANTIQUE TRÈS RARE FINE CHAMPAGNE

Tasting Notes

SIGNATURE PETITE CHAMPAGNE

Pale tawny core with wide lemon rim; oily, slightly unappealing nose; softening short fruit on palate with harsh final tones and short length. **Disappointing.**

RARE & DELICATE FINE CHAMPAGNE

Very light tawny core with wide pale green/lemon rim; light floral nose with no harsh tones; light short fruit on palate but lacks length and depth. **Fair.**

NAPOLÉON OLD RÉSERVE (DUTY-FREE)

Slightly deeper tawny hue than Rare & Delicate with distinct lemon rim; nose initially lacking, then soft light fruit with hint of smokiness; soft very light fruit on taste with harsh final edge and short length. **Fair.**

ANTIQUE "TRÈS RARE FINE CHAMPAGNE"

Pale tawny core with wide pale lemon rim; charming soft fruity nose with no harsh tones, appealing with a smoky hint; palate shows inviting good fruit and style with soft woody tones, mid-length. **Very good.**

1975 GRANDE CHAMPAGNE EARLY LANDED

(LANDED 1979, BOTTLED 1993 FOR THE BRISTOL BRANDY CO. LTD, BRISTOL)

Deep gold core with wide pale lemon rim; very light, delicate nose; fruity taste but with a harsh edge, lacking balance. **Fair to good.**

XO

(PACKED IN A TALL ELEGANT BOTTLE)

Deep tawny core with tight ocher rim; softening, quite rich mellow fruit on nose; fair fruit, softening, on palate but a harsh final edge. **Fair to good.**

EXTRA

(ELEGANT BOTTLE WITH VINE-LEAF MOTIF)

Same appearance as XO; fruity nose, quite rich with some honeyed wood; palate shows fair fruit, slightly clumsy and spirity though. **Fair to good.**

TRIOMPHE GRANDE CHAMPAGNE

Very pale tawny core with long gold rim; complex nose showing subtle fruit and oak overtones, which are appealing; fair fruit and spice on palate, mid-length. **Good.**

HINE

MAISON FONDÉE EN 1763

Edgard LEYRAT

LE DOMAINE CHEZ MAILLARD, 16440 CLAIX
TEL: (33-5) 45 66 35 72
Visitors Monday–Friday 5.30AM–12.30PM and 1.30–5.30PM

A family cognac business, Edgard Leyrat is the fourth generation and famous in gastronomic circles. The Leyrat vineyards are treated ecologically with no chemical fertilizers.

The vineyards cover 130.9 acres at Claix, southeast from Châteauneuf-sur-Charente and southwest from Angoulême, in the Fins Bois district. Most sales are in bulk. Leyrat maintains a stock equivalent of over 1 million bottles of maturing cognac.

Tasting Note

VSOP

Pale lemon hue; coarse, rather earthy fruit on nose; palate shows dull fruit, slightly harsh edge, mid-length.
Fair.

- RANGE -

VSOP

LEYRAT VSOP

Guy LHÉRAUD

DOMAINE DE LASDOUX, 16120 ANGEAC
TEL: (33-5) 45 97 12 33
Visitors from 9.00AM–12 noon and 2.00–5.00PM

*I*n 1680, Alexander Lhéraud started growing vines in the village of Lasdoux, near Cognac. In 1795, his son, Augustin, is known to have been cultivating 25 acres, let by the Lord of Bouteville, near Lasdoux, as a reward for taking care of his storehouse where today's cognac matures. Eugène Lhéraud, the great-grandfather of the present owner, secured a vineyard in the Grande Champagne district as a dowry in 1875 and six years later set up a still to sell cognac to the English market.

More land was acquired under Rémy Lhéraud in the 1930s. Guy Lhéraud took over in 1970 and started trading under his own label a year later, which now sells to such leading stores as the Richemond in Geneva and Harrods in London. Currently, 125 acres are farmed in the Petite Champagne, resulting in 106,000 gallons wine, planted 80 percent Ugni Blanc and 10 percent each of Colombard and Folle Blanche.

VSOP FINE PETITE CHAMPAGNE

Limousin oak is used to age the cognac with casks not less than eight years of age, apart from a small proportion of new for the raw spirit. About 150,000 bottles are sold annually. The Spécial has three years aging, the VSOP five years, the Cuvée 10 years, Cuvée 20 years, XO 30 years, and much longer for the Très Vieille Réserve du Paradis. Several cognacs are sold above 40 percent alcohol: Cuvée 10 at 42 percent, Cuvée 20 at 43 percent, XO at 44 percent, and Très Vieille Réserve du Paradis at 47 percent.

Sales are in Europe (including Germany, the U.K., Belgium, France, Luxembourg, and Denmark), Asia (Japan, Taiwan, Hong Kong, Malaysia), and the U.S.

Lhéraud has lovely packaging with period reproduction glass for deluxe lines. Several prizes have been won by Lhéraud. For the XO in 1996, they were awarded both a Commendation in the International Spirits Challenge and a silver medal in the Wine and Spirits Design Awards.

- **RANGE** -

SPÉCIAL

VSOP FINE PETITE CHAMPAGNE

CUVÉE 10

CUVÉE 20

XO

TRÈS VIEILLE RÉSERVE DU PARADIS

LHÉRAUD CUVEE 20

Tasting Notes

VSOP FINE PETITE CHAMPAGNE
(LOT NO 418)

Quite deep hue; damp wood nose, pecan nuts, rather spirity; raisons, slightly bitter taste with a final harsh edge. **Fair.**

CUVÉE 20 (43 PERCENT)
(LOT NO 341)

Mid-tawny; stylish nose, bitter chocolate; smooth palate, a shade too sweet but with good fruit and finish. **Very good.**

XO
(PACKED IN ATTRACTIVE EMBOSSED DECANTER WITH HIGH STOPPER)

Mid- to deep tawny core with light ocher rim; soft, smoky fruit on nose, rich with good extract; rich, good fruit and real depth on palate, tangerines, fair fruit. **Good to very good.**

J & F Martell

B.P. 21, PLACE EDOUARD MARTELL, 16101 COGNAC
TEL: (33-5) 45 36 33 33

Visitors (audio-visual in French, English, German, Italian, and Spanish from July–September on Monday–Friday at 9.30AM–5.00PM, Saturday–Sunday at 10.00AM–4.15PM; June–September on Monday–Friday at 9.30–11.00AM and 2.00–5.00PM, Friday at 9.30–11.00AM; and January–March and November–December on Monday–Thursday at 9.30–11.00AM and 2.00–5.00PM, and Friday at 9.30–11.00AM

Martell, the oldest of the major cognac houses, was founded by Jean Martell, who left his native home of Jersey in the Channel Islands to settle in Cognac in 1715. Born in 1694, the second youngest of eight children, Jean Martell's father was a navigator and merchant. After working with a merchant for seven years on the neighboring island of Guernsey, Jean Martell decided to try his luck in the Cognac region, aware of the potential in the region's spirit.

Martell's initial shipments were to Jersey and Guernsey, traditional trading posts "en route" to England. Trade with Rotterdam and the Hanseatic ports of Hamburg and Lubeck followed. By 1721, he was exporting over 53,000 gallons and seven years later purchased the land and buildings in Cognac which still house the company today.

Enthusiastic and energetic, Jean Martell regularly attended the local markets, visited the vineyard owners, and could often be seen at Tonnay-Charente personally supervising the loading of his barrels. Meetings with clients and agents took him to Orleans, Saumur, and other destinations beyond Cognac.

MARTELL CORDON BLEU

In 1726, Martell married the daughter of a cognac merchant, but he was widowed at an early age and remarried in 1737 to the daughter of an old Charentais family. He died in 1753, leaving a prosperous and reputable merchant house, whose control passed to his widow and two sons.

Martell's trade advanced with its first shipment to North America in 1784. Other landmarks included Martell's first export in bottle in 1797, its first shipment to Russia in 1803, and first mention of the "Extra" blend in 1819 when Théodore Martell wrote to his brother from London with an order for 15 barrels. The first shipment to London of Very Special Old Pale (Martell's first mention of VSOP) was in 1831.

- RANGE -

VS

MEDAILLON VSOP

NOBLIGE

NAPOLÉON SPECIAL RÉSERVE

CORDON BLEU

XO SUPRÊME

EXTRA

CLASSIQUE DE MARTELL

L'OR DE J&F MARTELL

CRÉATION DE J&F MARTELL

Martell exports started to Australia (1851), China (1861) and Japan (1868). However, a major setback occurred when the aphid, *phylloxera*, struck the vineyards of Cognac in 1880, destroying 80 percent of the vines. It took years to discover the solution of grafting European vines onto American resistant root stocks, followed by replanting, but then exports again took off.

The famous Martell blend, Cordon Bleu, was created in 1912. Martell was the cognac chosen on November 11, 1918, following the signing of the armistice. The company went public in 1975 and was purchased in 1988 by Seagram, the giant Canadian drinks company. New introductions followed: Napoléon "Special Réserve" in 1990, Gobelet Royal a year later, and L'Or in 1992, the latter presented in a prestigious 24-carat gold and glass decanter. Noblige was launched in 1994 and Création a year later, the latter to commemorate the 280th anniversary of the firm's foundation. The family is still closely involved, and Patrick Martell is president, the eighth generation to hold the position.

Today Martell owns over 700 acres under vine which includes 227.3 acres at Domaine de Gallienne – an estate in the Borderies district which was acquired in 1954. Yet all this land only contributes 3 percent of Martell's annual wine requirements. It has contracts with

CHÂTEAU DE CHANTELOUP

2,300 vine growers, many of whom the firm has worked with for over five generations. Stocks are purchased only from the top four districts, excluding Bons Bois and Bois Communs. Around 98 percent of the grapes are Ugni Blanc with tiny amounts of Colombard and Folle Blanche.

Martell's distillery at Gallienne claims to be the largest and most technically advanced in the region. It can distill 53,000 gallons wine per day, providing 30 percent of their needs. Thirteen independent distillers work exclusively for Martell, providing 47 percent of annual production, the balance being purchased from *bouilleurs de cru*.

The wine is not preheated in a *chauffe-vin* and is not distilled on the *lees*, either in its own 24 pot stills or the 140 under Martell's control in the 13 private distilleries.

At the second distillation, instead of accepting the spirit as low as 60 percent, Martell cuts off as high as 68 percent, thereby ensuring a drier style. It matures the young spirit at full strength and, when it is time to reduce, use a mix of cognac and distilled water ("faibles"), rather than water alone. The fine-grained Tronçais oak is preferred; it allows less evaporation and slower maturation than Limousin. Martell has its own coopers, who use staves that have aged for three years, before turning them into 90-gallon barrels. *Boisé* is added to boost both the lignin (for flavor) and tannin (for color).

Limousin oak is mainly reserved at Martell for repairing older barrels which are rejuvenated by introducing this type of oak which is much richer in tannin than Tronçais.

Martell sells over 21.6 million bottles annually and has one of the largest inventories in the region with the equivalent of over 100 million bottles in bulk stock. One of the key differences from other houses is its high use of Borderies: over 60 percent of the production of this district – the smallest of the six Cognac growths, lying to the north of the town and river – is reserved for Martell. This wooded and less chalky district imparts a sweeter and racier style to the brandy that is full-bodied with a hint of violets.

All but 2 percent of its sales are exported to over 140 countries; its worldwide share represents 17.5 percent of the cognac market. Martell claims to be first in the U.K., Italy, Mexico, Hong Kong, Malaysia, and Singapore.

Martell's most recent award was for the "Best Cognac of the Year" in 1997 for Création, given by *Wine & Spirit International*.

**MARTELL
XO
SUPREME**

For the future, the company has a new warehouse at Chanteloup with a capacity for 40,000 barrels, backed by an ambitious purchasing policy. Martell is at the forefront of research into the vineyard disease, *eutypiosis*, examining genetic engineering to produce disease-resistant genes that can be introduced into Ugni Blanc vines.

Martell has a busy reception center with 40,000 visitors annually, particularly in July and August.

It reserves the name Napoléon for a "special reserve" that is offered only on the duty-free market and is particularly popular in Asia.

Tasting Notes

VS

Pale tawny core with long, pale green rim appearance; rather spirity, farmy hot nose; clean, light fruit on taste, again slightly farmy, with short length. **Disappointing.**

MEDAILLON VSOP

(BEARING THE IMAGE OF LOUIS XIV, THE "SUN KING")

Quite deep tawny appearance with distinct, tight ocher rim; dull, soft fruit on nose; warming fruit with spirity finish on taste, mid-length. **Fair to good.**

NOBLIGE

(BEAUTIFULLY PACKED IN A CLEAR GLASS BOTTLE, LIKE A CRICKET BOWLING STUMP)

Mid-tawny core with long ocher rim; soft, warm fruit on nose; inviting, warm fruity taste, mid-length, spirity edge. Balanced. **Fair to good.**

CORDON BLEU

(AVERAGE 25 YEARS)

Mid-tawny core with wide, pale ocher rim; appealing, soft fruity nose with smoky hint; softening, good fruit on taste, mid-length. Balanced. **Good.**

XO SUPRÊME

(AVERAGE 30–35 YEARS, LAUNCHED 1987)

Mid-tawny core with wide, pale ocher rim; lovely, appealing smoky fruit on nose; inviting stylish, good fruit on palate but a slightly harsh final edge. **Good to very good.**

EXTRA

(AVERAGE 40 YEARS)

Pale tawny core with long ocher rim; soft, subdued and stylish nose; gentle soft palate showing light fruit and long length. Less appealing overall than the XO Suprême. **Good.**

L'OR

(MINIMUM 50 YEARS)

Mid-tawny core with tight, very watery ocher rim; complex, powerful fruity nose, showing slight smokiness – lacking the delicacy of Création as it contains more Borderies; rich, many-layered palate with peppery warm fruit, good length. **Very good.**

CRÉATION

(MINIMUM 50 YEARS)

Very soft, delicate nose, flowery suggesting acacia; soft, lovely elegant taste with no harsh tones and long length. **Exceptional.**

Jean-Paul MAURIN

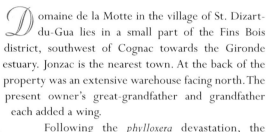

DOMAINE DE LA MOTTE, 17240 ST. DIZANT-DU-GUA
TEL: (33-5) 46 49 96 28
Visitors by appointment from Monday–Saturday at 9.00AM-7.00PM

$\mathcal{D}$omaine de la Motte in the village of St. Dizart-du-Gua lies in a small part of the Fins Bois district, southwest of Cognac towards the Gironde estuary. Jonzac is the nearest town. At the back of the property was an extensive warehouse facing north. The present owner's great-grandfather and grandfather each added a wing.

Following the *phylloxera* devastation, the vineyard was replanted and Maurin's grandfather constructed a larger warehouse for maturing cognac to the east of the property. The old distillery adjoined the house and now has been sited behind, thereby facilitating supervision of the process.

The vineyard is on two sites: 34.6 acres of white grapes and 5 acres of red grapes at la Motte and 14.8 acres white grapes at St.

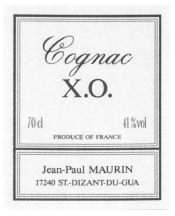

Bonnet, which lies south but still within the Fins Bois designation. Only Ugni Blanc is cultivated for the cognac but Colombard, Merlot, Malbec, and Cabernet Sauvignon are grown for Pineau des Charentes (both white and rosé). The soil is mostly clay/chalk, imparting a distinct scent to the young cognac and a taste of hazel nuts, according to Maurin. About 53,000 gallons wine is made annually.

- RANGE -

FINE FINS BOIS

VSOP

VIEILLE RÉSERVE

XO

Maurin is a *bouilleur de cru*, maturing the spirit in Tronçais oak from the Vicard cooperage which is not less than 12 years old. *Boisé* is added. Between 15,000–20,000 bottles cognac are made annually. The Fine Fins Bois is matured for four years and is said to be very scented; its fiery style makes it appropriate as a cocktail base. The coarseness has lessened with the VSOP whose length on the palate is achieved by seven years in cask. The Vieille Réserve is aged for 15 years to obtain a delicate, yet full nose. The XO is over 40 years old and sold at he slightly higher alcoholic strength of 41 percent. It is not filtered in order to retain its natural state.

Tasting Note

JEAN PAUL MAURIN
VIEILLE RÉSERVE

Mid tawny core with distinct mid ocher rim appearance; smoky fruit, woody on nose; palate shows softening woody fruit, several layers with good length. Appealing and balanced.
Good.

MÉNARD et Fils

B.P. 16, 16720 St. Même-les-Carrières
tel: (33-5) 45 81 90 26
Visitors from Monday–Friday at 9.00AM–12 noon, and 2.00–6.00PM

*T*he Ménard family owns official papers from around 1660 which show that the parents of Nicolas Mesnard (the surname was written with an "s" until the mid-nineteenth century) plowed the land and possessed both a press and stills in the small village of Salles d'Angles west of Segonzac in the Grande Champagne district. A succession of Ménards, all bearing the Christian name of Jean, labored on the same land for almost three centuries.

By 1815, the family owned a substantial vineyard and were known to be distillers. This has provided the Ménards with a treasure trove of old stocks, dating back to three bottles from before the French Revolution of 1789, followed by "hundreds of bottles" from the 1818 and 1830 vintages.

In 1946, Jean Paul Ménard, together with his two sons, Guy and Pierre, decided to sell their own cognac and bottle Pineau des Charentes. The latter is in three forms: white and rosé, both of about three years, and a 10-year-old whose "quality has practically no equivalent on the market," according to Ménard.

Today its vineyard covers 197.6 acres entirely composed of Ugni Blanc vines, which yield about 148,400 gallons, entirely of Grande Champagne status. No grapes, wine, or immature spirit are purchased in. It

MÉNARD VSOP GRANDE FINE CHAMPAGNE

distills at both Mainxe (south of Jarnac) and at Ambleville (northeast of Archiac).

The Ménard warehouse is at St. Même-les-Carrières, which lies between Jarnac and Châteauneuf-sur-Charente. Limousin oak is used from the Pelletant cooperage in Mainxe and another in Segonzac with an average age of 20 years, 5 percent of which is new. The alcoholic reduction depends upon the aging intended to be given to the cognac; old brandies will reach 60 percent naturally. The Ménards like to respect tradition, eschewing non-natural ways to speed up the process.

> **· RANGE ·**
>
> SÉLECTION DES DOMAINES
>
> VSOP
>
> NAPOLÉON
>
> XO
>
> ANCESTRALE

Annually 38,000 bottles are sold: 8,000 bottles Sélection des Domaines, 25,000 bottles VSOP, and 5,000 bottles of the higher qualities. It has been known for cognac at Ménard to stay in wood for over 70 years in certain cases to ensure high quality blends. Its stocks equate to over a half-million bottles.

Exports are to Germany, the Netherlands, Belgium, and Malaysia. Various generations have praised Ménard cognacs. In 1900, it won a medal for quality at the Universal Exhibition in Paris.

There are five cognacs in the Ménard range. The Sélection des Domaines (corresponding to Three Stars) is two to five years, while the VSOP is 4–10 years. The Napoléon is a superior cognac of 20–25 years. While these are sold at 40 percent alcohol by volume, the two top levels are of higher strength: XO at 42 percent is about 35 years, while Ancestrale at 45 percent is 50 years old. The latter is known for its *rancio* (taste of wood), according to Ménard.

Tasting Note

MÉNARD GRANDE FINE CHAMPAGNE VSOP

Pale tawny core with bright ocher rim development; nose shows elegant fruit, quite flowery; stylish, good fruit, many layered palate, slightly spirity finish with fair acidity, mid length.
Good to very good.

MENUET

B.P. 24, 16720 St. Même les Carrières
tel: (33-5) 45 81 99 78
Visitors from 9.00am–12 noon and 2.00–6.00pm

The Menuet family can trace its first vineyard to 1680 in the Cognac region. In 1850, Louis Menuet enlarged his holding with 12.4 acres in the Grande Champagne district.

Today Menuet has 98.8 acres, all planted with Ugni Blanc, in the Grande Champagne, based on the village of St. Même les Carrières in the northeast of the district between the towns of Cognac and Châteauneuf-sur-Charente. Picking normally starts on October 15, and runs for three weeks. This is the northern limit for cultivating the

MENUET XO
GRANDE
CHAMPAGNE

Ugni Blanc. They make 95,400 gallons wine from its own vineyards, with no grapes, wine, or spirit purchased in. The wine is kept on its *lees* for one month to ensure more aroma development prior to distillation in its 663-gallon copper Charente still.

The raw spirit is placed at full strength in new Limousin oak, obtained from Seguin Moreau, for one year and then transferred into older barrels. From its second year, the cognac is slowly reduced in strength by 5 percent over several stages until it reaches 45 percent six months before bottling. The final sales strength is 40 percent for the annual production of 130,000 bottles.

Sixty percent of Menuet is exported, principally to Japan, but other sales are made to Hong Kong, Taiwan, Thailand, the U.K., Belgium, Germany, and the Netherlands. In the U.S., it is sold under the "Menuet & Jules" label. They concentrate on specialist shops, clubs, and restaurants.

This "Premier Cru de Cognac" was recognized in 1900 when Ernest Menuet (Louis's grandchild) secured a gold medal at the Universal Exhibition in Paris. In 1993, they obtained a silver award for their XO at the International Wine and Spirit Competition in London, while in 1996, the VSOP and XO secured silver and gold medals at the Chicago-based Beverage Testing Institute awards.

Today the sixth generation presides. André Menuet's daughter, Marie-Josette, married Michel Croizet. Their son, David, together with his wife, Christine, look after the commercial and marketing aspects.

Menuet VSOP spends five years in oak, securing flowery and vanilla tones, while the XO is said to show coffee, cinnamon, honey, orange blossom, and vanilla – a delicate blend "between the fruit age and the oak age," according to David Croizet. Over 20 years of aging is given to Extra, reminding tasters of cacao and crystallized fruits in addition to vanilla, coffee, and wood flavors. The Hors d'Age is kept at least 40 years in oak to ensure a complex and harmonious style.

- RANGE -

VSOP Grande Champagne

XO Grande Champagne

Extra Grande Champagne

Hors d'Age

Tasting Note

MENUET XO GRANDE CHAMPAGNE
(PRESENTED IN A LOVELY DECANTER, ALMOST HEART-SHAPED)

Pale tawny core with long lemon rim appearance; nose shows soft fruit, subtle, almonds; dried fruit on taste, shortish length, lacks richness but is delicate.
Very good.

J.Y. & F. MOINE

VILLENEUVE, 16200 CHASSORS
TEL: (33-5) 45 80 98 91
*Visits to the distillery depart from the tourist office in Jarnac at 2.30PM,
Saturday and Sunday by appointment*

*J*ean-Yves and his brother, François, Moine took over the family business in 1979 and started selling cognac in bottle in 1986. They sell only their own production: 70 percent cognac, 20 percent Pineau des Charentes (white and rosé) and 10 percent local wine under the Vins de Pays Charentais designation.

The Moines vinify about 84,800 gallons wine, which is entirely Ugni Blanc for cognac. Merlot and Cabernet grapes are grown for the Pineau rosé and Vin de Pays rosé and red, while the Chenin Blanc is used in the Vin de Pays and Pétillant de Raisin.

At Villeneuve, near Jarnac, they distill 663 gallons, aging in 8- to 10-year-old Limousin oak casks supplied by the Joseph Gatard cooperage at Sigogne. About 1,200 bottles Réserve Cognac of 8 years are made annually and 1,000 bottles of 18-year-old Vieille Réserve. Sales are both at the property and with specialists, both in France and in Belgium.

- RANGE -

RÉSERVE

VIEILLE RÉSERVE

MOINE FRÈRES RESERVE

The Moines have won several awards for their eco-tourism initiatives, including the 1993 Challenge National du Tourisme Vert, 1994 Bravos de l'acceil, and the 1996 Grand Prix Banque Populaire.

Tasting Note

MOINE FRÈRES RÉSERVE

Light hue — pale straw appearance; spirity, citrus fruit nose; light fruit on palate, thin, spirity edge. **Disappointing.**

FRANÇOIS AND JEAN-YVES MOINE

CHECKING THE DISTILLING PROCESS

MOINE FRÈRES VIEILLE RESERVE

Château MONTIFAUD

17520 JARNAC
TEL: (33-5) 46 49 50 77
Visitors Monday–Friday 9.00AM–12 noon and 2.00–6.00PM.
Weekends by appointment

Château Montifaud has been owned by the Vallet family for several generations, stretching back three centuries. It maintains old stocks that are kept under cover in half-light. Some 79,500 gallons date back to 1947.

The 123.5-acre vineyard lies in the Petite Champagne district. The prefix château is little seen in Cognac and is reserved for the properties belonging to ancient families of the region. The cognac is bottled at the property.

Two stills at Château Montifaud distill wine made from the Ugni Blanc grape. The spirit is matured in new Limousin oak for

- **RANGE** -

VS PETITE
CHAMPAGNE

VSOP PETITE
CHAMPAGNE

NAPOLÉON
PETITE
CHAMPAGNE

XO
FINE PETITE
CHAMPAGNE

XO FINE PETITE
CHAMPAGNE

six months and then transferred to old casks. All are eventually reduced to 40 percent alcohol.

The VS is five years old of which one year is spent in a young cask; no *boisé* is applied. The VSOP is aged 10 years, again with one year in young wood. Napoléon is 15–18 years on average, while the XO has a 27–30 years' maturation.

The major market is the Netherlands, but exports are also made to Germany, the U.K., Denmark, Belgium, Austria, Norway, and Sweden. A bottle of Heritage Maurice Vallet from Cognac distilled around 1900 was auctioned by Christie's at the 1987 Vinexpo.

Tasting Notes

VS FINE PETITE CHAMPAGNE

Pale straw hue; sweetish, delicate, lime-blossom aroma; sweetish fruit on palate. **Good.**

VSOP FINE PETITE CHAMPAGNE

Deep ocher appearance; very spirity nose; initially smooth taste with evident vanilla. **Fair to good.**

XO FINE PETITE CHAMPAGNE

Mid-gold core with pale ocher rim; peaches and dried flowers on nose, a shade spirity; softening, subtle fruit on palate with hard finish, mid-length. **Fair to good.**

CHÂTEAU MONTIFAUD, FINE PETITE
CHAMPAGNE

MOYET

62 RUE DE L'INDUSTRIE, 16104 COGNAC
TEL: (33-5) 45 82 04 53
Closed in August

The company was started in 1864 by Euthrope Moyet and traded particularly successfully from 1900–1940 but then declined. A single cellar master looked after the blending for over 60 years until Moyet was purchased in 1979 by Pierre Dubarry and Marc Georges. Since 1982, it has regained its former reputation for quality, particularly its emphasis on very old stocks. Today it is stocked by 1,100 restaurants in Paris, together with distribution by Nicolas, and sold by 26 exporters around the world.

Moyet owns no vineyards, preferring to buy both immature spirit straight off the cognac still and some mature spirit. Its sources are 50 percent Grande Champagne, 35 percent Petite Champagne, 10 percent Borderies, and 5 percent from other districts. Dubarry prefers the distillation to take place off the *lees* and mainly uses Tronçais wood, particularly for the new oak.

MOYET BORDERIES

When the alcoholic reduction is required, a mix of cognac and distilled water is applied slowly in four or five stages. About 70,000 bottles are sold annually. The main export markets are the East Coast of the U.S., Germany, Taiwan, Thailand, and Italy. Moyet rarely participates in competitions, but in 1995 it entered the U.K.-based International Wine & Spirit Competition, securing gold, silver, and bronze awards.

In addition to the maturing casks in central Cognac, older reserves are held in glass demijohns at a warehouse north of the town of Cognac.

Dubarry and his business partner, Georges, administer Moyet from Paris but make frequent visits to Cognac. They eschew terms like Three Star and VS.

- **RANGE** -

PETITE CHAMPAGNE

FINE CHAMPAGNE

BORDERIES

FINE CHAMPAGNE
XO

GRANDE
CHAMPAGNE

GRANDE
CHAMPAGNE EXTRA
VIEILLE

PETITE CHAMPAGNE
TRÈS VIEILLE

BORDERIES TRÈS
VIEILLE

FINE CHAMPAGNE
TRÈS VIEILLE

GRANDE
CHAMPAGNE TRÈS
VIEILLE

MOYET PETITE CHAMPAGNE

Tasting Notes

PETITE CHAMPAGNE
(ORANGE LABEL)

This major-selling cognac for Moyet is an average seven years old, showing light, clean fruit on nose and balanced, soft fruit on palate with mid-length. **Fair to good.**

FINE CHAMPAGNE
(PALE GREEN LABEL)

Twelve years old with inviting warm, soft fruit on nose; appealing, nutty, fruity palate. This was the original cognac of the house. Today it is a blend of Grande and Petite Champagnes, reduced at 11 years prior to one year's final maturation. **Good to very good.**

FINE CHAMPAGNE XO

Soft, elegant, fruity nose; palate shows many-layered, walnut, soft, stylish fruit, reflecting its 30–35 years of age. **Very good.**

BORDERIES

Nose shows rich, mellow fruit; palate is warming, rather heavier than other cognacs in the range. 35 years old from two farms, one providing 70 percent. **Good.**

GRANDE CHAMPAGNE
EXTRA VIEILLE

With an average 35–40 years, of which a quarter of a century has been spent maturing at one farm, the nose shows warm, soft, stylish fruit; good, inviting fruity taste, long, rich finish with no harsh edges. **Very good.**

FINE CHAMPAGNE
TRÈS VIEILLE

Over 50 years old, soft, lovely, fruity nose; quite rich, honey and hazel-nut palate. **Very good.**

GRANDE CHAMPAGNE
TRÈS VIEILLE

Over 50 years old, including 1848 vintage, this is a blend of four ages, the youngest being 1906; fine, soft, stylish nose; lovely, soft, elegant, fruity palate, good length. **Very good to exceptional.**

J. NORMANDIN-MERCIER

CHÂTEAU DE LA PÉRAUDIÈRE, 17139 DOMPIERRE
TEL: (33-5) 46 68 00 65
Visitors from 9.00AM–12 noon and 2.00–5.00PM all year

The house was founded in 1872 by Jules Normandin, a cognac owner and broker. He purchased Château de la Péraudière for its old warehouse and to develop his blending trade. Mercier was his mother-in-law who became his business partner. His son, Edward, succeeded and, in time, his son, George.

Péraudière lies almost 5 miles east of the port of La Rochelle. From 1945–1978, the House sold cognac only in barrel as *négoçiants* for the large houses. Since then Normandin-Mercier has sold in bottle, both in France and abroad, presided over by the fifth generation, Jean-Marie Normandin.

- **RANGE** -

FINE PETITE CHAMPAGNE

VIEILLE FINE CHAMPAGNE

GRANDE CHAMPAGNE
RÉSERVE

TRÈS VIEILLE GRANDE
CHAMPAGNE

PETITE CHAMPAGNE VIEILLE
47 DEGREES

GRANDE CHAMPAGNE VIEILLE
43 DEGREES

FINE CHAMPAGNE PRESTIGE

CHÂTEAU DE LA PÉRAUDIÈRE, NEAR LA ROCHELLE.

While the family owns land, none is in the company's name. Purchases are 60 percent Grande Champagne and 40 percent Petite Champagne. The immature spirit is not reduced in strength for five years. Maturation is 70 percent in Tronçais oak and the balance selected by the cooper. The policy is to place the new cognac in new wood for about eight months and then transfer it to old casks. Vicard and Seguin Moreau supply the barrels.

Two cognacs are sold above 40 percent: Petite Champagne Vieille at 47 percent and Grand Champagne Vieille at 43 percent. The Très Vieille Grande Champagne reaches 40 percent naturally without any water reduction. The higher-strength cognacs account for 10 percent of sales.

The main export markets are the U.S., Germany, Switzerland, Australia, Spain, Denmark, and Japan. In addition to cognac, Normandin-Mercier sells a white and rosé Pineau des Charentes.

- **RANGE** -

FINE PETITE
CHAMPAGNE

VIEILLE FINE
CHAMPAGNE

GRANDE
CHAMPAGNE
RÉSERVE

TRÈS VIEILLE
GRANDE
CHAMPAGNE

PETITE CHAMPAGNE
VIEILLE 47 DEGREES

GRANDE
CHAMPAGNE VIEILLE
43 DEGREES

OTARD

CHÂTEAU DE COGNAC, 127 BOULEVARD DENFERT
ROCHEREAU, 16100 COGNAC
TEL: (33-5) 45 36 88 88

*Open Monday-Friday all year round except Christmas day. Weekend opening
from April through September*

*B*aron Jean Baptiste Antoine O'tard de Lagrange, cofounder of Otard Cognac, was born in Brives, near Cognac, in 1763 of Norwegian, Scottish, and French descent. He secured an engineering diploma from military college and married into an old French–Canadian family in 1792. Caught up in the French Revolution, he was condemned to death in 1793, but on the eve of his execution, he was rescued from prison by the local people.

Otard was forced to emigrate and went to England, returning in 1795 to join Jean and Léon Dupuy, friends and neighboring land-owners, in establishing an export trade in cognac, using the old stocks he had.

The business was so successful that they purchased Château de Cognac as their base the following year. The property had been rebuilt around 1450 by Count Jean de Valois, who had been a prisoner for 33 years in England. The future king of France, François I, was born there in 1494, and the Château remained a royal property until 1789. However, it had been much neglected and was even turned into a prison to house English

NAPOLÉON EXTRA FINE

soldiers taken during the Seven Years' War (1756–63).

Château de Cognac had ideal conditions for maturing cognac owing to the thickness of the walls (6.6 feet) and floors–particularly the drier parts for young spirit–and the damp cellars close to the river Charente for older cognac. With Dupuy as distiller and Otard as salesman, it proved a winning partnership. George III of Britain had permission to have their cognac exported despite the Continental embargo.

Otard was popular locally, being elected mayor of Cognac in 1804 until his death 20 years later, living then in the house which today is the Town Hall. Twice he was elected Member of Parliament, in 1820 and 1824, as well as being awarded the Legion of Honor. After Otard's death and Jean Dupuy's retirement, Léon Dupuy and Otard's sons managed the business. Their descendants continued the trade, changing the name from the original Otard-Dupuy in 1945 to Cognac Otard when the Dupuy family was no longer represented. In 1991, it was acquired by Martini & Rossi, which in turn merged with Bacardi the following year.

Otard owns no vineyards, preferring to purchase about 185,500 gallons young spirit from four districts: 10 percent from the Borderies and 30 percent each from Fins Bois, and

Grande and Petite Champagne districts, mainly from the Ugni Blanc grape. Otard contracts with 500 vine-growers and 10 distillers, some of whom store the young cognac for two to four years. Michel Larcade, cellar master at Otard and nephew of the former one, prefers the distillation to be undertaken with the *lees*, especially in the top two districts of Grande and Petite Champagne. He dislikes the *chauffe-vin* because the spirit can pick up off-flavors.

If a spirit is required for relatively short aging, it is matured at a higher alcoholic strength, such as 65 percent, but Otard reduces to 55 percent if the cognac is intended to have a long cask life. *Boisé* is added to adjust the wood supplied because the "toasting" of the casks is not uniform. Limousin oak is used, just 5 percent of which is new, bought from three cooperages in the Cognac region.

About 40 percent of the Otard stock is aged at Château de Cognac. This includes its treasured old reserves, which are housed in a former

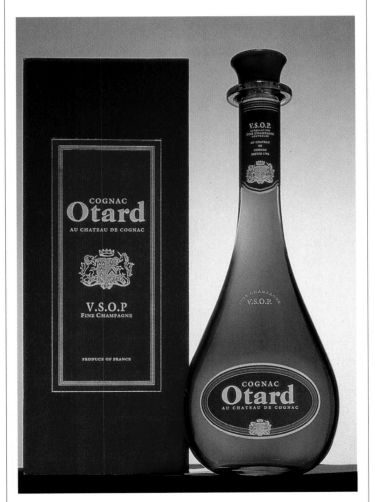

VSOP FINE CHAMPAGNE

prison, known today as the "Paradise." The vintages stretch back to the nineteenth century, such as 1820 (with a smoky nose like fine old Madeira combined with soft, lovely fruit), 1878, 1902, 1906 (showing supple, rich, lovely fruit), and 1924 (with intense fruit and *rancio* richness). The really old stocks are held in glass demijohns, just three of which exist from the 1820s. The alcoholic strength during exposure to the air in cask means that the 1924 is now 45 percent, the 1906 around 38 percent and the 1820 down to 32–33 percent.

After blending, the cognac is placed in a large vat of about 4,770 gallons prior to bottling. The length in this vat varies: three months (VS), six months (VSOP), one year (Napoléon) and 18 months (XO).

Otard has won several notable awards: the gold medal in 1995 at the Plovdiv Bulgarian International Fair and twice at the U.K.-based

OTARD ADVERTISING "OTARD DUPUY, THE BEST OF THE
WORLD. WHAT A PITY NOT TO BE ABLE TO DRINK IT." (1920s)

OTARD ADVERTISING "KNIGHT OF OTARD'S BRANDY." (1925)

International Wine & Spirit Competition, with the silver in 1994 and bronze award in 1996.

Over the years, Otard has excelled with the style and dramatic effect of both its advertising and packaging. In 1996, a metal box illustrating the distinctive tear-shaped bottle was launched. A Mexican advertisement in 1920 showed a diver discovering a bottle of Otard but frustrated that he could not taste the treasure on the seabed.

Today some 10,000 visitors a year visit Château de Cognac. Note particularly the courtyard where one can see the "mullioned" windows of the room where François I was born, as well as the state banqueting hall and guards' room; these rooms still carry the graffiti of the English and Irish prisoners held there during the Seven Years' War.

Tasting Notes

VSOP

Nose shows spice and vanilla; softening fruit on palate with a slightly harsh edge.
Fair to good.

NAPOLÉON

Stylish, rich, warming, dried-fruit nose; rather spirity, rich taste, slightly fiery finish.
A blend of the top four districts.
Good.

XO

Nose shows real depth with aromas of leather, spice, and dried fruit, stylish; softening, very fruity taste, mid-length. A blend of mainly Grande and Petite Champagne with some Borderies.
Good to very good.

EXTRA

Lovely, warming, soft fruit, elegant nose; supple palate showing softening apricots and walnuts, long length.
Very good to exceptional.

J. PAINTURAUD

3 RUE PIERRE GOURRY, LE PEUX, 16130 SEGONZAC
TEL: (33-5) 45 83 40 24/45 83 42 77
Visitors all year

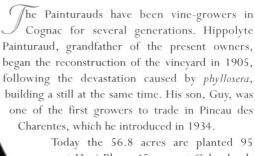

*T*he Painturauds have been vine-growers in Cognac for several generations. Hippolyte Painturaud, grandfather of the present owners, began the reconstruction of the vineyard in 1905, following the devastation caused by *phylloxera*, building a still at the same time. His son, Guy, was one of the first growers to trade in Pineau des Charentes, which he introduced in 1934.

Today the 56.8 acres are planted 95 percent Ugni Blanc, 45 percent Colombard, and just 0.5 percent Montils. The vineyard lies entirely within the Grande Champagne district, regarded as the premier cru (first growth) of cognac.

About 66,250 gallons wine are distilled on site in a 663-gallon capacity still. Two coopers in the village of Segonzac supply casks: 80 percent from the Limousin forest and 20 percent Tronçais. New oak is used for the first 7–9 months of the spirit, and it is

VIEILLE RÉSERVE GRANDE CHAMPAGNE

then transferred into casks with an average age of 12 years. The alcoholic strength is reduced slowly by about 5 percent per annum.

Painturaud makes about 6,000 bottles cognac of which 40 percent is VSOP, 25 percent Réserve, and 30 percent Vieille Reserve. Sales are 85 percent within France, 5 percent to Benelux states, and 10 percent in the rest of Europe. They also sell 9,000 bottles Pineau des Charentes, which has been selected by the *Guide Hachette* each year since 1993; the Pineau range is Blanc, Rosé, and 10 years old.

- **RANGE** -

VSOP GRANDE CHAMPAGNE

RÉSERVE GRANDE CHAMPAGNE

VIEILLE RÉSERVE GRANDE CHAMPAGNE

HORS D'AGE GRANDE CHAMPAGNE

COGNAC
GRANDE CHAMPAGNE
APPELLATION GRANDE CHAMPAGNE CONTRÔLÉE

J. PAINTURAUD S.A.R.L
LE PEUX 16130 SEGONZAC FRANCE

0.70 ℓ   PRODUCE OF FRANCE   40 % vol.

LE COGNAC EST LE PRODUIT DE LA DISTILLATION DE VINS RÉCOLTÉS DANS LA RÉGION DÉLIMITÉE ET CIRCULANT SOUS TITRE JAUNE D'OR DE LA RÉGIE.

Tasting Note

VIEILLE RÉSERVE GRANDE CHAMPAGNE

Distinct, mid-tawny core with light, pale ocher rim; nose is most appealing, showing hazelnuts and wood smoke; fair fruit, quite rich palate, apricots, good length and high extract; a little fiery on final finish. **Good.**

Château PAULET

26 RUE DU DOMINANT, B.P. 24, 16101 COGNAC
TEL: (33-5) 45 32 07 00
Visitors by request to (33-5) 45 32 07 00 from Monday–Friday

XO FINE
CHAMPAGNE

*C*hâteau Paulet was founded in Jarnac in 1848. It is independent and family-owned. Today it is run by the fourth generation of the Lacroux family (Bernard and Jacques).

Annually, Château Paulet purchases about 26,000 gallons young cognac from the Grande and Petite Champagne, Fins Bois, and Borderies. It has no vineyards of its own. New Limousin oak–mainly from the Seguin Moreau–is used, but older barrels are employed for maturing older cognac. Cognacs are reduced with a blend of cognac and distilled water.

About 120,000 bottles are sold each year under the Château Paulet label. In addition, the company owns Barnett (established 1869), Dubois, (established in Jarnac in 1848), and Tricoche (founded 1820). An important part of

Tasting Note

CHÂTEAU PAULET XO FINE CHAMPAGNE
(FROSTED BOTTLE WITH VERY LONG NECK)

Amber hue; stylish fruit, apricots, many layers on nose; palate shows elegant fruit, tangerines, slightly fiery final edge, good length, balanced. **Very good.**

its trade is supplying own label to prestigious retailers (such as Harrods, Fauchon, Marks & Spencer). Its major markets are Europe (the U.K., Belgium, Germany, Luxembourg, Italy, the Netherlands, Portugal), Far East (particularly duty-free), and North America/Mexico. Among the lovely packaging is Lalique crystal for its very rare Fine Champagne. Its VS Three Star makes up 50 percent of their sales, VSOP Réserve is 25 percent, and the older qualities are 25 percent.

Château Paulet has won several awards for the XO Fine Champagne including both the gold medal and Cyril Ray Trophy in 1993 (for the XO Fine Champagne) and again the gold medal in 1996 at The International Wine & Spirit Competition, held in the U.K.

- **RANGE** -

ECUSSON ROUGE
FIVE STAR

VSOP

CUVÉE SUPÉRIEURE

NAPOLÉON EXTRA

CUVÉE EXCELLENCE

XO FINE
CHAMPAGNE

BORDERIES TRÈS
VIEILLES

CARAFE XO

RESERVE LOUIS XVI

LALIQUE

ECUSSON ROUGE FIVE STAR

André PETIT et Fils

16480 BERNEUIL
TEL: (33-5) 45 78 55 44
*Visitors from Monday–Friday at 8.00AM–12 noon and 2.00–6.00PM;
Saturday mornings for groups by appointment*

*A*round 1850, the grandfather of the present owner's grandmother, M. Goulard, a weaver by trade, purchased a vineyard and built a distillery with the advice of his cousin, a worker in the Hennessy plant. In 1921, the vineyard's name was changed to Petit on the marriage of Albert Petit into the family.

Until 1965, André Petit (the present generation's father) sold his output to Hennessy but in that year decided to bottle his spirit. Eighty percent of current requirements are supplied from its own vines, which lie in the Fins Bois and Petite Champagne districts. They are still harvested by hand. The yield is about 25,970 gallons wine. Some 265–530 gallons young spirit is bought in.

Two stills are used at the distillery at Berneuil, which lies in the Fins Bois between Saintes and Pons, just off the N137 road. The young cognac is reduced to 60 percent alcohol. Limousin oak is used, with the wood varying in age from new to 25 years.

The Three Star is four years old. Although youthful, Petit aims to enrich the floral aromas with wood tones. They recommend it for

ANDRÉ PETIT XO

cocktails. The mellower VSOP (8–10 years old) has dominating vanilla characteristics, while the 15-year-old Vieille Réserve Napoléon should show finesse and distinct *rancio* character. Petit says the latter has "a slightly smooth taste reinforced by a radiant vivacity–to be tasted in a moment of peace and serenity."

The Très Rare XO is 25 years old; Petit aims to produce a delicate but exceptionally complex nose where the *rancio* mingles with aromas of "under-growth, vanilla and old prunes," according to the firm. It aims for a round, smooth texture. Hors d'Age is its top of the range, the Réserve Familiale: a blend of old cognac that is rich with aromas of jasmin and tobacco leaves and well balanced on the nose; the taste should release delicate oak flavors.

In addition to cognac, Petit make both white and rosé Pineau des Charentes. The white is aged for six years in oak barrels and is recommended to serve in place of Sauternes with dessert. The rosé spends less time in cask and makes an appealing apéritif.

Most of Petit's cognac sales are in Belgium, Germany, South Africa, and Taiwan. A silver medal was awarded at the 1990 Mondiale.

> - RANGE -
>
> THREE STAR
>
> VSOP
>
> VIEILLE RÉSERVE NAPOLÉON
>
> TRÈS RARE XO
>
> HORS D'AGE

Tasting Note

XO

Mid-tawny hue; elegant, fruity nose with hint of jasmin; peppery fruit with fair length on palate. Balanced. **Very good.**

PLANAT

29 RUE MARGUERITE DE NAVARRE, 16100 COGNAC
TEL: (33-5) 45 32 28 28
*Visitors May–October Monday–Friday 10.00am–12 noon and 2.30–4.30pm;
otherwise by appointment*

*E*stablished in 1828, Planat is a recognized *eleveur* of old and fine cognacs. Oscar Planat, son of the founder, was also a politician and became mayor of Cognac in 1878. He went on to receive "la Croix de la Legion d'Honneur" and had one of the main streets in Cognac named after him. Planat was purchased in the early 1960s by Jean Paul Camus of the illustrious Camus family, vineyard owners and leading *négociants*.

The house style is a floral spicey aroma and rich, warm, smooth flavor "with a touch of that typical Cognacaise fire." Only Limousin oak is used for maturing the cognac.

- **RANGE** -

VSOP

VIEUX COGNAC DE
PETITE CHAMPAGNE
RÉSERVE DES
CONNOISSEURS

TRÈS VIEUX COGNAC DE
PETITE CHAMPAGNE

GRANDE CHAMPAGNE
RÉSERVE EXTRA VIEILLE

1972 GRANDE
CHAMPAGNE

1966 FINS BOIS

TRÈS VIEUX
COGNAC DE
PETITE
CHAMPAGNE

Tasting Notes

VSOP

Shows a mid-gold core with light, pale rim; earthy, heavy fruit on the nose; rich, heavy fruit on palate with a rather spirity edge.
Disappointing.

VIEUX COGNAC DE PETITE CHAMPAGNE RÉSERVE DES CONNOISSEURS

Pale ocher rim and mid-gold appearance; soft, fruity nose; slightly harsh but fruity edge on palate with mid-length. **Fair.**

TRÈS VIEUX COGNAC DE PETITE CHAMPAGNE

Deep gold core with mid-pale lemon rim; fair, supple fruit, quite rich and heavy on nose; raisony fruit, fairly rich and supple on palate with mid-length. **Fair.**

GRANDE CHAMPAGNE RÉSERVE EXTRA VIEILLE

Tawny core and light, pale-lemon rim; nose has fair style with soft, fruity richness; rich, heavy fruit on palate with mid-length. **Good.**

1972 GRANDE CHAMPAGNE

(BOTTLED MARCH 18, 1996)

Mid-straw core with light, pale rim; surprisingly youthful nose with light fruit; softening light fruit also on palate, but a harsh final edge. **Fair.**

1966 FINS BOIS

(BOTTLED MARCH 18, 1996)

Pale- to mid-straw; rich, lovely, fruity nose with many layers; palate shows softening, hearty fruit with balanced acidity; medium length. **Very good.**

VIEUX COGNAC DE PETITE CHAMPAGNE RÉSERVE DES CONNOISSEURS

PRUNIER

7 AVENUE DU GÉNÉRAL LECLERC, 16100 COGNAC
TEL: (33-5) 45 35 00 14
Visitors Monday–Thursday 8.00–11.30AM and 1.00–2.00PM.
Friday 8.00–11.30AM. Weekends by appointment

Jean Prunier (1665–1732), a "freeman" of the Cognac port of La Rochelle, was the first member of the Prunier family to ship wines and cognac around 1700. He was succeeded by his son, Gabriel (1711–1790), and his grandson, Jean (1741–1804). The family acquired vineyards in Cognac around St. Jean d'Angély, and François Prunier (1768–1843) moved in the early nineteenth century to the town of Cognac to be closer to them. He started to build up today's premises.

A successor, Alphonse Prunier, died in 1918, leaving the family with no direct descendant. His widow, Camille, called on her nephew, Jean Burnez (1897–1969), to take over the management. His son and daughter now represent the major shareholders.

Today Prunier owns no vineyards or stills but purchases about 7,950–10,600 gallons immature cognac, derived from Fins Bois (60 percent), Grande Champagne (25 percent) and Petite Champagne (15 percent). Prunier aims to maintain the authenticity of their cognacs, aging and blending them. It is proud to still be independent.

New Limousin oak is used, but the average oak of the casks is 10 years old. The Sansaud cooperage in Segonzac in the Grande Champagne district supplies the casks. About 500,000 bottles are sold annually: 60 percent

FAMILY RÉSERVE XO

VS/Three Star, 20 percent VSOP and the balance in superior qualities. In the early 1970s, Prunier increased its exports to the Far East and its major sales are now to Taiwan, the U.K., Belgium, the Netherlands, Japan, Hong Kong, and Germany. In Cognac, there is a carefully restored medieval property, owned by Prunier, known as the Maison de la Lieutenance. For many years, it was the official residence of the lieutenants general of Cognac. Prunier has taken the "Old House" as its trademark.

Recently Prunier was awarded the gold medal for its Très Vieille Grande Champagne XO in San Francisco.

The Family Réserve has been part of the range for over 20 years. The blend (from the Grande and Petite Champagne districts and Fins Bois) is achieved after long oak maturation. The cognacs range in age from 15–25 years old. Claud Burnez, with good stock inventories, was able to persuade the authorities of the age of 20 years old and receive special exemption to place this information on the label for Prunier "20 year old."

- **RANGE -**

VS

THREE STAR

DE LUXE

VSOP

NAPOLÉON

FAMILY RÉSERVE XO

TRÈS VIEILLE
GRANDE
CHAMPAGNE

20 YEARS OLD

Tasting Notes

FAMILY RÉSERVE XO

Mid-tawny, rather deep color; fruity, woody nose; fair fruit but too spirity, mid-length. Disappointing.
Fair.

20 YEARS
(FROM THE 1969 AND 1970 VINTAGES, BOTTLED 1994)

Pale hue; mid-straw core with long watery lemon rim; delicate wood smoke and some apricots on nose; firm fruit on palate, high quality, mid-length, though slightly fiery edge.
Very good.

RAGNAUD-SABOURIN

DOMAINE DE LA VOÛTE, 16300 ABLEVILLE
TEL: (33-5) 45 80 54 61
Visitors Monday–Friday 9.00AM–12 noon and 2.00–5.30PM

*T*he Ragnaud-Sabourin vineyard was acquired in 1850. Around 1945, Gaston Briand–who was president of the Cognac Growers' Association–decided to market his own cognac. Today the house is predominantly managed by his lady descendants: Denise (Gaston Briand's daughter), Annie (her daughter), and Patricia (Annie's daughter), with help from their husbands, Marcel Ragnaud, Paul Sabourin, and Xavier Rief respectively.

One hundred and twenty-three and a half acres in the Grande Champagne district provide the base, with no blending spirits from other deistricts. Almost all is planted with Ugni Blanc except a small plot of Folle Blanche which has been replanted. The spirit is aged only in Limousin oak, because they consider Tronçais does not release tannin quickly enough. The freshly distilled cognac spends a maximum nine months in new wood with no *boisé* added and no chill filtration, which can result in a haze. Most of the cognac is matured at 60 percent alcohol.

Ragnaud-Sabourin has a faithful following. At the estate at Ambleville, which lies almost equidistant between Segonzac and Barbezieux, substantial stocks amounting to 15–17 times their annual requirements are held to ensure mature blends are available. No caramel is added to adjust the color.

All of the cognacs are sold above the usual cognac strength of 40 percent. The Grande

RAGNAUD-SABOURIN GRANDE CHAMPAGNE

Champagne is at least four years old, reduced in strength two to three months after leaving the pot still. It is released at 41 percent alcohol, as is the VSOP, which is 10 years old. Both the Réserve Spéciale (20 years old) and Fontvieille (35 years old and named after the oldest part of the vineyard) are 43 percent alcohol. Florilège reaches 46 percent alcohol naturally over its life of 45 years. The Héritage Ragnaud is a blend of three vintages (1902–04) and, like Le Paradis, sold at 41 percent. The latter is a subtle blend of 90 percent cognacs from around 1900 and 10 percent from pre-1870 distillations.

- **RANGE** -

GRANDE CHAMPAGNE

VSOP

RÉSERVE SPÉCIALE

FONTVIEILLE

FLORILÈGE

HÉRITAGE RAGNAUD

LE PARADIS

Tasting Notes

GRANDE CHAMPAGNE

Pale straw color; good, inviting, fruity, warm nose; rich, many-layered taste, good length, but slightly harsh final edge. **Good.**

VSOP

Mid-straw / pale gold appearance; subtle, lovely, fruity nose combined with vanilla; fair fruit on palate but distinct, harsh edge and short length. **Fair to good.**

RÉSERVE SPÉCIALE

Mid-straw / pale gold hue; nose lacking but showing delicate fruit; warming, good, fruity palate, several layers and spirity edge. **Good.**

FONTVIEILLE

Mid-gold appearance; lovely, stylish fruit combined with rich honey on nose; soft, rich, elegant palate, long length, some rancio *character.* **Very good.**

FLORILÈGE

Mid-gold appearance with long ocher rim; complex dried fruit on nose, rich and many-layered; palate shows warm, spirity fruit, again many-layered, mid-length. **Very good.**

LE PARADIS

Mid-gold core with wide, pale lemon rim on appearance; very soft, lovely fruit and style on nose; palate shows soft, stylish fruit with citrus touches, balanced, long length. **Very good to exceptional.**

Raymond RAGNAUD

LE CHÂTEAU, 16300 AMBLEVILLE
TEL: (33-5) 45 80 54 57
Visitors from 8.00AM–12 noon and 1.30–5.30PM

*P*aul Ragnaud took on Château d'Ambleville in the heart of the Grande Champagne district in 1920. After his death in 1941, his son, Raymond, developed the vineyard and made fine old cognacs. Since his death in 1963, his wife and two children (Jean-Marie Ragnaud and Françoise Bricq) have increased the area under vine to 108.7 acres. It all lies within the premier cru (or first growth) Grande Champagne: Ambleville, Hauteneuve, and Chez Cormier.

Some 148,400 gallons wine are made, all from the Ugni Blanc grape, and passed through two stills to produce 10,600 gallons cognac.

- RANGE -

SÉLECTION

RÉSERVE

VIEILLE RÉSERVE

GRANDE RÉSERVE

RÉSERVE RARE

EXTRA VIEUX

HORS D'AGE

TRÈS VIEILLE
GRANDE
CHAMPAGNE

HÉRITAGE

EXTRA
VIEUX

This is matured in Limousin oak, yielding about 45,000 bottles after evaporation.

Nine different qualities of cognac are made: Sélection at three to four years age; Réserve, seven years; Vieille Réserve, 41 percent alcohol and 15 years; Grande Réserve, 44 percent alcohol and 15 years; Réserve Rare, 41 percent alcohol and 18 years; Extra Vieux, 42 percent and 25 years; Hors d'Age, 43 percent alcohol and 35 years; Très Vieille Grande Champagne from 1952 at 50 percent alcohol, and Héritage from 1906 at 45 percent alcohol.

Sales are in Germany, Belgium, Switzerland, Italy, the U.K., and Japan. The company should not be confused with Ragnaud-Sabourin, also in Ambleville. Some of France's leading restaurants stock Ragnaud cognacs, including La Tour d'Argent, Ritz and Miraville in Paris, Crocodile (Strasbourg), and Carlton (Cannes).

A six-year-old Pineau des Charentes is also produced, which Ragnaud recommends serving as an apéritif.

Tasting Notes

RAYMOND RAGNAUD EXTRA VIEUX GRANDE FINE CHAMPAGNE

Pale tawny core with long pale lemon rim; elegant, many layered nose, prunes; palate shows hazelnuts, soft fruit, many layers, stylish, long length.
Very good.

RÉMY MARTIN

20 RUE DE LA SOCIÉTÉ VINICOLE, 16102 COGNAC
TEL: (33-5) 45 35 76 00
Visitors all year with train tours from April–October

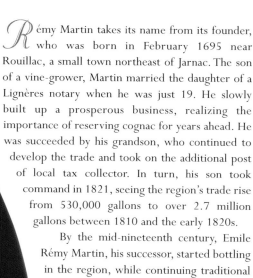

*R*émy Martin takes its name from its founder, who was born in February 1695 near Rouillac, a small town northeast of Jarnac. The son of a vine-grower, Martin married the daughter of a Lignères notary when he was just 19. He slowly built up a prosperous business, realizing the importance of reserving cognac for years ahead. He was succeeded by his grandson, who continued to develop the trade and took on the additional post of local tax collector. In turn, his son took command in 1821, seeing the region's trade rise from 530,000 gallons to over 2.7 million gallons between 1810 and the early 1820s.

By the mid-nineteenth century, Emile Rémy Martin, his successor, started bottling in the region, while continuing traditional sales by the barrel. He thought up their logo, a centaur, and registered their first trademarks in 1874—just prior to the problems caused in the vineyards by the aphid, *phylloxera*; this devastated production, which fell in the region from 3.7 billion gallons in 1875 to under half in three years. In turn, Paul Rémy Martin established the brand in Australia,

VSOP FINE CHAMPAGNE

Scandinavia, and the U.S., but almost bankrupted the business with his lifestyle.

Rémy Martin was saved by André Renaud, the son of a Grande Champagne grower, who concentrated the firm's trade on distilling from a smaller area–the launch of VSOP Fine Champagne in 1927. The designation "Very Superior Old Pale" was an eighteenth century term for old cognacs. He had seen the appellation law on regional origin in 1919 and decided to apply a brand based on two districts. Sales took off with the energetic help of Pierre Rivière in Paris and Otto Quien on export markets. From 1936, the prestigious Louis XIII blend was presented in a Baccarat crystal decanter. By Renaud's death in 1965, the company had built up substantial stocks and was selling 300,000 cases a year–the leader in the superior quality cognac market.

Rémy Martin realized that to expand it required even greater stocks, although already for every bottle sold, eight bottles were

- RANGE -

VS
VSOP
Superieur
Club
Napoléon
XO Special
Extra
Limoges
L'Age d'Or
Louis XIII

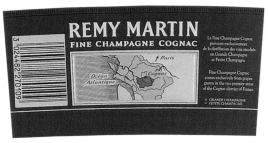

maturing in bulk in its warehouses. Grower associations were encouraged. The first contract to supply was in 1966 for 265,000 gallons from 250 farmers. Twenty years later, the same Champaco cooperative has 2,000 growers, representing 19,760 acres. A lovely promotional idea for special visitors was developed at the same time: to present a living vine and annually to send not only an economic and vineyard report but also a check for the vine's net revenue—usualy 10 to 80 centimes, depending upon the year! This certainly helped to spread the word.

Renaud's successor, André Heriard Dubreuil, had a modern production unit built outside Cognac in the late 1960s and saw the introduction of a frosted bottle for the VSOP. In 1970, the largest cooperage in Europe, turning out 30,000 barrels a year or a quarter of France's production, was constructed under the Seguin-Moreau name, using only Limousin oak. New quality levels were introduced: Napoléon (aimed at the Japanese market), XO, and Extra between VSOP and Louis XIII.

Today the cognac house is listed on the Paris and Frankfurt stock exchanges and has acquired three champagne houses (Krug, Charles Heidsieck, and Piper-Heidsieck), and the Bordeaux merchant, De Luze. A merger with Cointreau was effected in 1990.

Rémy Martin owns only 494 acres, which supplies around 3 percent of their needs. Some 1,800 vine-growers are contracted. The vast

REMY MARTIN VSOP ON ICE

XO
SPECIAL

majority of the wine distilled is Ugni Blanc with small quantities of Colombard and Folle Blanche. The firm has four distilleries at Gensac, Juillac, St. Même, and Touzac. Prior to oak-aging, all qualities (apart from cognac intended for the Louis XIII blend) are reduced with demineralized water to 60 percent alcohol.

Usually, Limousin oak barrels of 93 gallons are filled, but occasionally a *tierçon* (146 gallons) is employed; the maximum capacity legally is 186 gallons. The cellar master, Georges Clot, is experimenting with a little Russian oak. All the barrels are supplied from its sister company, Seguin-Moreau.

Annual sales are some 20 million bottles: 60–65 percent VSOP and the balance in other qualities, but all at 40 percent alcohol. Exports are to over 165 countries with major sales to China, Japan, Vietnam, Singapore, Taiwan, the U.S., Canada, Germany, the U.K., the Netherlands, and Austria. Its most recent award was the gold medal at the 1996 Sélections Mondiales in Montreal, Canada, for the XO Spécial Fine Champagne Cognac.

Its distilling methods include preheating the wine in a *chauffe-vin*, having ensured that the wine passes through its malolactic fermentation and distilling on the *lees* to increase the fruitiness of the spirit, particularly on the aroma.

Typically VSOP is seven years, Napoléon 15–17 years, XO 21 years, Extra (for the duty-free market) 30 years, and Louis XIII over half a century in age.

CELLAR MASTER GEORGES CLOT AT WORK.

CARAFE LOUIS XII

Tasting Notes

VSOP

Nose shows quite heavy fruit; palate is mid-fruitiness, mid-length and a spirity edge. **Fair to good.**

LOUIS XIII

Rich, lovely fruit, very stylish nose; supple, rich palate, soft, many-layered with no harsh tones, mid-length. **Very good.**

RENAULT BISQUIT

DOMAINE DE LIGNÈRES, 16170 ROUILLAC
TEL: (33-5) 45 21 88 88
Visitors from June–September

*A*lexandre Bisquit was just 20 years old when he founded his own cognac house in 1819. He was an adventurous trader, sometimes escorting his barrels as far as the China Sea. At other times, Bisquit was to be found on Sundays on the quayside in Jarnac, rewarding the maker of the best cask with a five franc gold coin–quite a small fortune in those days; this gesture earned him the very best barrels.

In modern times, Renault merged with Castillon in 1963; in 1991, the combined company joined the Pernod Ricard group. Bisquit merged with Paul Ricard in 1965, which became Pernod Ricard in 1974. The group's cognac business has been known as Renault Bisquit since 1991.

Today Renault Bisquit is the only major cognac house to have its entire production and sales operation on one site. This brings together the distillery (which is the largest in the Charente region), cooperage, cellars, bottling plant, and administration on a 852.2-acre estate, which lies in the Fins Bois district near the small town of Rouillac (northeast of Jarnac). Within the property of Château de Lignères, 506.4 acres are under vine. The site is 525 feet above sea level, ensuring the vines bud slightly later than elsewhere and suffer less from

RENAULT CARTE NOIR EXTRA

spring frosts. The Renaissance-style château lies in the middle of a park of century-old trees.

The grapes at Lignères account for only 12–18 percent of Renault Bisquit's needs, depending upon the vintage. The modern distillery houses 64 stills–so large that the stillman bicycles around the modern installation during the crucial five months following the wine's fermentation. Even during Christmas and New Year, the double-pot still distillation continues day and night. The *lees* are not included. To retain more of the fruit, the residue from the second distillation is mixed with the *brouillis*.

The raw spirit is placed in barrels, 70 percent derived from Tronçais and the balance from Limousin oak. The casks are made in Renault Bisquit's own impressive cooperage with each craftsman making three 93-gallon barrels a day, using about 30 staves a barrel. Although the regulations say the staves should be dried for three years before use, the house keeps them for five years.

Jacques Rouvière has been cellar master at Bisquit for over 20 years. He says, "A good Charente native drinks his father's cognac and prepares his son's." A renowned oenologist, Rouvière's experience and intuition ensure a consistency and style to the Renault Bisquit ranges. The old stocks–dating back to an 1819 Grande Champagne, the year Bisquit was founded –give added depth to younger cognac.

The traditions of the two merged houses is substantial. Bisquit was the cognac of both King George VI and Winston Churchill; the latter would apparently take no other cognac to accompany his Double Corona cigars.

- RANGE -

BISQUIT THREE STAR CLASSIQUE

BISQUIT VSOP FINE CHAMPAGNE

BISQUIT PRESTIGE FINE CHAMPAGNE

BISQUIT NAPOLÉON FINE CHAMPAGNE

BISQUIT PASSION VSOP

BISQUIT XO EXCELLENCE FINE CHAMPAGNE

BISQUIT EXTRA GRANDE CHAMPAGNE

BISQUIT L'ETERNITÉ GRANDE CHAMPAGNE

BISQUIT PRIVILÈGE D'ALEXANDRE GRANDE CHAMPAGNE

BISQUIT FLEUR

BISQUIT CAMARADE

BISQUITE CHÂTEAU DE LIGNÈRES VIEILLE RÉSERVE PRIVÉE

RENAULT CARTE NOIRE EXTRA

RENAULT CARTE D'ARGENT EXTRA

Tasting Notes

BISQUIT RANGE THREE STAR CLASSIQUE

Some states call it Three Star (such as France and Switzerland) and others "Classique." Nose shows quite soft fruit; palate rather fiery edge.
Fair.

VSOP FINE CHAMPAGNE

Nose shows inviting, warm, soft fruit; palate has softening fruit, mid-length but quite spirity. **Good.**

NAPOLÉON FINE CHAMPAGNE

Nose has very soft, appealing, warm fruit; palate is clean with soft fruit, mid-length but still slightly spirity on final taste.
Good to very good.

XO EXCELLENCE FINE CHAMPAGNE

Nose is very soft, stylish, and elegant; palate is of high quality, showing lovely elegance and mid-length.
Very good.

EXTRA GRANDE CHAMPAGNE

Rich, many-layered, fruity nose; rich, good fruit on palate, mid-length; balanced. **Very good.**

L'ETERNITÉ GRANDE CHAMPAGNE

Smoky, very soft, appealing nose; palate is soft, many-layered, subtle and very stylish with good length.
Exceptional.

PRIVILÈGE D'ALEXANDRE GRANDE CHAMPAGNE
(90 TO 100 YEARS BUT MINIMUM 80 YEARS)

Rich, good fruit with many layers on nose; warming, lovely fruit with long length on palate. It reaches 41.5 percent alcohol by volume quite naturally with no water addition and no sugar added.
Exceptional.

CHÂTEAU DE LIGNÈRES VIEILLE RÉSERVE PRIVÉE

Soft, light fruit on nose; palate shows stylish, soft fruit with no harsh tones. No caramel added and only 10 percent of the vineyard's crop goes into this cognac.
Good to very good.

RENAULT CARTE NOIRE EXTRA

Accounts for four-fifths of Renault's sales. Nose shows rather heavy, soft fruit; palate also heavy, soft, fruity style, mid-length and somewhat clumsy finish.
Fair.

RENAULT CARTE D'ARGENT EXTRA

Warm, subtle, good fruit on nose; very soft palate with no harsh edge, fairly dry, mid-length.
Good to very good.

Louis ROYER

27–29 RUE DU CHAIL, B.P. 12, 16200 JARNAC
TEL: (33-5) 45 81 02 72
Visitors by appointment

*L*ouis Royer was brought up in Jarnac in a house bordering the Charente river. At an early age, he acquired an intimate knowledge of the vineyards and the wine-making and distillation processes; by the time he was 20 he had become a cellar master. In 1853, Royer, 24 years old, founded his own cognac house on the site where he grew up, building a warehouse and, shortly afterwards, a cooperage and distillery. Four generations have succeeed him. In 1989, the business was purchased by Suntory. Today, Louis Royer has a staff of 58, an annual turnover of 260 million French Francs, and is the seventh

largest house in the cognac market. It is identified by its symbol, the bee.

Louis Royer has no vineyards but purchases 2.1 million gallons wine from the Ugni Blanc grape and 132,500 gallons immature cognac from the Fins Bois and Grande and Petite Champagne districts. It has one distillery at Aumagne in the Charente Maritime

LOUIS ROYER XO

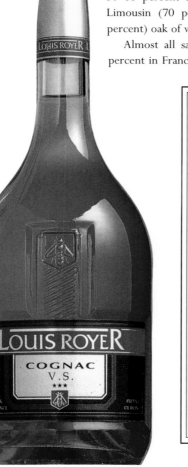

and also purchases old cognacs from *bouilleurs de cru*.

The cognac is reduced in strength to 50–55 percent alcohol for maturation in Limousin (70 percent) and Tronçais (30 percent) oak of which 5 percent is new.

Almost all sales are exported (only 1 percent in France), amounting to 662,500

- **RANGE** -

LOUIS ROYER
VS/THREE STAR

LOUIS ROYER VSOP

LOUIS ROYER
NAPOLÉON

LOUIS ROYER XO

JULES DURET VS

JULES DURET
VSOP

JULES DURET XO

PIECE D'OR
NAPOLÉON

PIECE D'OR
NAPOLÉON EXTRA

ARBELON VS

ARBELON VSOP

LOUIS ROYER VS

gallons to Europe, Hong Kong, Taiwan, Singapore, and South Korea. The bronze medal was won for their XO at the 1996 Séléctions Mondiales held in Montreal and gold medal for the same cognac at the 1992 Concours de Spiriteux in Lausanne. The XO is a blend of Grande and Petite Champagne with Borderies.

Tasting Note

LOUIS ROYER XO

(PRESENTED IN ATTRACTIVE SQUARE-SHAPED DECANTER WITH HEAVY STOPPER)

Appearance of mid-tawny core with wide, pale lemon rich; rim, many-layered nose with good extract, showing vanilla and hazel nuts; rich, good, fruity palate, lively style, fairly smooth, mid-length. **Very good.**

LOUIS ROYER VSOP

M. TIFFON

B.P. 15, 16200 JARNAC
TEL: (33-5) 45 81 08 31

M.Tiffon was founded in 1875 by Méderic Tiffon, trading in bulk to Scandinavia. It owns 98.8 acres in the Grande Champagne and Fins Bois districts, which yield 119,250 gallons. In addition, it purchases white wine from about 350 vine-growers. In total, this means its cognacs are 10 percent Borderies and 30 percent each from Fins Bois and the Grande and Petite Champagne districts.

TIFFON VSOP FIINE CHAMPAGNE

Tiffon has 10 pot stills in Jarnac. It matures the spirit 70 percent in Allier oak and the balance in Tronçais, purchasing from the Vicard cooperage. Its total stock of 15,000 casks equates to 12 million bottles.

Its major sales are 150,000 bottles VS, 30,000 VSOP, 10,000 Napoléon, and 5,000 XO. Above VS, the blends are from the two best cognac districts of Grande and Petite Champagne. The two highest qualities are blended at Château de Triac by Philippe and Antoine Braastad.

- RANGE -

VS

VSOP

NAPOLÉON

XO

VIEUX SUPÉRIEUR

GRANDE CHAMPAGNE

TIFFON XO
FINE
CHAMPAGE

Tasting Notes

TIFFON VSOP FINE CHAMPAGNE

Deep amber-gold, distinct mid-ocher rim; appealing, good fruit, coffee on nose; supple, fiery fruit, some style on palate; good length.
Good.

TIFFON XO FINE CHAMPAGNE
(ATTRACTIVELY PRESENTED IN AN OVAL BOTTLE, EMBOSSED WITH ENCIRCLING CURVES)

Mid-tawny core with distinct, mid-gold rim; nose shows many-layered, rich rancio fruit, good wood development; good fruit, many layers on palate, rich extract, good length, balanced, stylish.
Very good.

TRIJOL

2 Impasse du Paradis, 17520 St. Martial sur Né
TEL: (33-5) 46 49 53 31
Visitors from Monday–Friday by appointment

*I*n September 1859, the Trijol family became cognac vineyard owners and distillers, a tradition that has since passed through five generations. Today, the combined companies of Maxime Trijol and Duboigalant are headed by Jean Jacques Trijol, based at St. Martial sur Né, northwest of Archiac in the Petite Champagne.

Just 3 percent of Trijol's wine requirements come from its own 98.8 acres vineyards, which are equally split between the Grande and Petite Champagne districts. The Grande Champagne property is at Salle d'Angles, west of Segonzac, and the Petite Champagne at both Archiac and St. Martial sur Né, south of Celles. Its own land supplies about 79,500 gallons. Some 2.1 million–2.7 million gallons wine is purchased annually and 132,500 gallons immature cognac. Ugni Blanc accounts for 99 percent with the balance in Folle Blanche. About 30 percent each comes from Grande and Petite Champagnes and Fins Bois with 10 percent originating in the Borderies.

Its distillery is equipped with 18 Charente pot stills. The spirit is aged in Limousin oak of which about a quarter is new, purchased from Seguin Moreau and other coopers. The average cask oak is eight years. In

TRIJOL VSOP

addition to its activity as a *bouilleur de cru*, Trijol sells several cognacs under its own label or that of its associate house. Trijol matures the VS at 67 percent, VSOP at 62 percent, VSOP Supérieur at 58 percent, and XO (which is intended to be a very old cognac) at 50 percent alcohol. The strength is reduced by adding distilled water. No *boisé*, sugar, or syrup solutions are used.

Trijol recommends its VS and VSOP as long apéritifs and both the VSOP Supérieur and XO to be served as digestifs. VS accounts for about 120,000 bottles, VSOP 60,000 bottles, VSOP Supérieur 30,000, and XO (packed in an elegant bottle with tapering neck) 15,000 bottles. Many European and southeast Asian countries import Trijol cognacs.

- RANGE -
TRIJOL VS
TRIJOL VSOP
TRIJOL VSOP SUPÉRIEUR
TRIJOL NAPOLÉON
TRIJOL XO
DUBOIGALANT VSOP
DUBOIGALANT VSOP SUPÉRIEUR

The XO Maxime Trijol won the 1996 bronze award at The International Wine and Spirit Competition held in the U.K.

Its associate house, Duboigalant (*see page 104*), has a fine range, produced exclusively from the Grande Champagne vineyards belonging to the Trijol family. Duboigalant is named after one of the vineyard plots.

Tasting Notes

VSOP

Pale lemon; coarse, rather hot fruit on nose; coarse, hot, fruity palate with short length.
Disappointing.

VSOP SUPÉRIEUR

Mid-ocher hue; elegant, fruity nose; good fruit, butterscotch, with good length; balanced.
Good to very good.

MAXIME TRIJOL XO
(ATTRACTIVE DECANTER EMBOSSED WITH FLEUR-DE-LYS)

Mid-tawny core, water-lemon rim; nutty, soft, light fruit on nose, quite appealing, second nose shows vanilla; rich, mellow, hot, slightly peppery finish on palate. **Good.**

UNICOOP

49 RUE LOHMEYER, B.P. 35, 16102 COGNAC
TEL: (33-5) 45 82 45 77
Visitors July 1–September 15 daily from 9.00AM–12.30PM and 1.30–7.00PM.
April 1–June 30 and September 16–30 from 10.00AM–12 noon and
2.30–6.00PM except Wednesday, Saturday, and Sunday.
Guided tours in English

The Union Coopérative de Viticulteurs Charentais represents over 1,000 vine-growers, sunflower producers (Europe's largest), and livestock farmers. Its cognac members are based 45 percent in Fins Bois, 35 percent in Bons Bois, and 20 percent in the three districts of Borderies, and Grande and Petite Champagne. The cooperative was established in 1929. It sells 6.25 million bottles of which 70 percent is exported.

Unicoop has 11 distilleries with 60 stills, annually distilling 6.6 million gallons. Maturation takes place in 32,000 barrels and 250 larger vats of 3,975–13,250 gallons each. Its stock of 2.1 million gallons pure alcohol equates to 28 million bottles.

Unicoop likes to preheat the wine in a *chauffe-vin* but prefers to distill off the *lees*. A syrup adjustment is made at the final

PRINCE HUBERT DE POLIGNAC VSOP

blending stage within a year of bottling. Maturation is half in Limousin oak and half in Tronçais.

The cooperative also controls Henri Mounier, a company established in 1858. This is based at Le Laubaret, 2.5 miles from Cognac and has a bottling capacity of 76,000 bottles per day.

For cognac, Unicoop uses several labels for its sales in 65 countries, but Prince Hubert de Polignac is the main brand. Unicoop also sells Pineau des Charentes

(2.5 million bottles, 40 percent exported) and regional wine.

Polignac takes its name from one of France's oldest noble families which can be traced to the ninth century. Among its members have been Cardinal de Polignac (ambassador in Poland and Rome in the seventeenth century), Duchess Yolande de Polignac (a close friend of Marie-Antoinette in Louis XIV's reign), and Prince Jules de Polignac

(Charles X's Minister). Prince Hubert de Polignac gave his name to H. Mounier for a cognac and, in turn, Mounier has given Unicoop the same rights as well as the use of the family's motto and coat of arms.

Tasting Notes

PRINCE HUBERT DE POLIGNAC VSOP

Soft, fruity nose; softening fruit on palate, rather harsh final edge, short length. **Fair.**

PRINCE HUBERT DE POLIGNAC DYNASTY

Heavy fruit on nose; palate lacks style with fruit that appears not to be unified, harsh final edge, mid-length. **Fair.**

PRINCE HUBERT DE POLIGNAC XO ROYAL

(PRESENTED IN LOVELY DECANTER)

Deep gold core with light lemon rim; warm, firm, fruity nose, tobacco hint, a shade spirity; supple, fruity taste, mid-length; final fiery edge, balanced. **Fair to good.**

Glossary

ALEMBIC A still.

BNIC Bureau National Interprofessionnel du Cognac (the controlling body for cognac).

BOISÉ Infusion of oak resin/shavings placed in cognac to enhance its woody character.

BONNE CHAUFFE Second distillation.

BOUILLEUR Distiller.

BOUILLEUR DE CRU Vineyard owner who distills his own crop, some of which may be sold to cognac houses but increasingly such distillers are selling under their own names.

BOUILLEUR DE PROFESSION Trade distiller who distills different growers' wines.

BROUILLIS First distillate, which takes about 12 hours to make.

CHAI Warehouse for maturing cognac.

CHAUDIÈRE Boiler.

CHAUFFE-VIN Tank to preheat wine before distillation, reducing heating costs and helping to maintain the copper still but resulting in oxidized wine if the temperature rises too high.

COEUR DE CHAUFFE Heart or middle run of the distillation.

COPEAU DE BOIS Wood chips.

EARLY LANDED Young cognac shipped in bulk, usually of a single vintage, which matures in the bonded warehouses of the importing country, usually the U.K.

EAU DE VIE Any spirit but generally referring to grape brandy.

EUTYPIOSIS Fungus *Eutypa armeniacea*, first identified in 1977: airborne fungal spores enter the vine through wounds left by pruning; this develops into a canker, shriveling the leaves and flowers, reducing grape yield, and eventually poisoning the plant with the toxin, eutypine.

FAIBLES Blend of cognac and distilled water, used to reduce alcoholic strength, around 15–18 percent by volume.

FINE CHAMPAGNE Blend from the Grande and Petite Champagne districts of Cognac where not less than half originates in the former.

LEES Residue of skins and pips from fermentation.

MALOLACTIC Second fermentation when malic acid is converted into lactic acid.

OIDIUM Vine disease first identified in the 1850s.

PARADIS Storage point for the oldest cognac reserves.

PHYLLOXERA Aphid that devastates vines, both in winged and subterranean form, seen in Cognac in early 1870s, requiring growers to graft onto resistant American rootstocks.

RANCIO Characteristic nose and taste of fully mature cognac–a mellow quality found after some 20–25 years in cask; some call it a Madeira fragrance.

TONNELIER Cooper.

VS Very Special.

VSOP Very Superior Old Pale.

XO Extra Old–a term retained for higher-quality cognacs.

Index

Index

Index

Picture Credits

The Publisher would like to thank Fortnum & Mason, Piccadilly, London for making bottles of cognac available for photography. The Publishers would also like to thank the following for permission to reproduce their photographs in the book:

p13 Janet Price, p16 © Remy Martin Cognac; p17, 18, 20 Hennessy; p22 (top) © Remy Martin Cognac; p22 (bottom) Bureau National Interprofessional du Cognac (BNIC); p24 (top) Martell; p24 (bottom),p25 © Remy Martin Cognac; p26 BNIC; p27 Martell; p28, 29 Hennessy; p30 Château de Cognac; p31, 32 (top) Hennessy; p32 (bottom) Delamain; p35 Hennessy; p38, 39 SIPPA and BNIC; p40 BNIC; p41, 42 Château de Cognac; p43 Janet Price; p44–7 Comite regional du tourisme; p202, 204, 205 © Remy Martin Cognac.

Author's Thanks

In writing this book, I should particularly like to thank Claire Coates and Susie Lyddon (Bureau National Interprofessionnel du Cognac), Rupert Gregory (who accompanied me to Cognac), Christian Thomas (Château de Beaulon), Jean-Paul Camus (Camus), Jean-Marc Olivier and Ivor R Braastad (Courvoisier), Alain Braastad-Delamain (Delamain), Max and Béatrice Cointreau and Olivier Paultes (Frapin), Gillian Green (French Tourist Office), Paul-Jean Giraud (Paul Giraud), Michael Longhurst and Philip Juniper (Hennessy), Bernard Hine (Thomas Hine), Pierre Dubarry (Moyet), Michel Larcade and Aude Rocourt (Otard, Gaston de Lagrange, Exshaw), Georges Clot and Françoise Lapeyre (Rémy Martin), Jacques Rouvière and Kristina de la Ferrière (Renault Bisquit), Ian Harris (Seagram UK), Marcus Strodijk (Unicoop), and my tasting panel: Spencer and Susan Batiste, Alan and Valerie Beardmore, Helen and Rupert Gregory, Ray and Gina Marks, Edward and Carol Pope, and Keith and Lois Pope.